HOT Chile
Cookbook

**Hot and fiery recipes
from spicy world cuisine**

JACKIE

THOUGHT OF YOU WHEN I SAW THIS BOOK

HOPE YOU GET ALOT OF GOOD USE OUT OF IT

BON APPETIT

UNCLE RICCONE

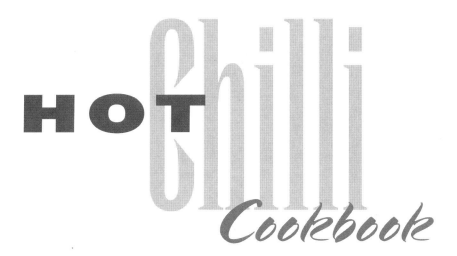

HOT Chilli Cookbook

**Hot and fiery recipes
from spicy world cuisine**

Edited by Jenni Fleetwood

KNICKERBOCKER
PRESS

A QUINTET BOOK

Published by Knickerbocker Press
276 Fifth Avenue, New York, New York 10001

This edition produced for sale in the U.S.A., its
territories and dependencies only.

ISBN 1-57715-027-9

This book was designed and produced by
Quintet Publishing Limited
6 Blundell Street
London N7 9BH

Creative Director: Richard Dewing
Art Director: Clare Reynolds
Designer: John Strange
Project Editor: Doreen Palamartschuk
Editor: Jenni Fleetwood
Illustrator: Shona Cameron

Typeset in Great Britain by
Central Southern Typesetters, Eastbourne
Manufactured in Hong Kong by
Regent Publishing Services Ltd.
Printed in Hong Kong by
Sing Cheong Printing Co. Ltd.

CONTENTS

Introduction	7
Global Guide to Fresh and Dried Chiles	8
Powders, Pastes, and Sauces	12
Using Chiles	14
Dips and Snacks	17
Soups	37
Appetizers	49
Fish and Seafood	63
Poultry	79
Meat Dishes	105
Vegetarian Choice	133
Salads and Vegetables	159
Sauces and Salsas	173
Pickles and Chutneys	181
Index	191

INTRODUCTION

PIQUANT, PUNGENT OR packing a powerful punch, chiles are valued by cooks the world over for the flavor they provide, and although they have been traditionally associated with hot countries, they are becoming increasingly popular in cooler climes, thanks to international travel and improved marketing. Visit a supermarket in Stockholm, Wellington, or Washington and you are likely to find fresh chiles on the vegetable racks, dried chiles and chili powder with the spices and hot pepper sauces and salsas alongside other condiments.

Chiles have been cultivated for centuries, ever since the ancestors of today's Mexicans discovered a species of wild capsicum which not only tasted good, but treated their tastebuds to a whole new sensation. From the initial spark, the species evolved rapidly, and today there are more than two hundred different varieties of chile, ranging in strength from mild to extremely hot.

The Aztecs were very fond of chiles, and it is reputed that the emperor Montezuma had his cooks prepare thirty different dishes every evening, many of them spiked with one or more types of his favorite flavoring.

Early Spanish and Portuguese explorers were seduced by the charms of chiles and took the brightly colored flavorings with them when they left the shores of Central and Southern America. Soon chiles were being grown in North and West Africa, in Madagascar and throughout India, where they were seized upon with delight, as an alternative to black pepper, which had been the favored spice up to that time.

Chiles rapidly reached China, where they were to become an important part of Szechuan cuisine, and also spread to South-east Asia. Thailand, Vietnam, and Korea embraced the chile with enthusiasm, valuing it as much for its appearance as its flavor.

Today chiles are cultivated wherever conditions permit, although the major producers continue to be Mexico, the American states of New Mexico, California, Texas, Arizona, and Louisiana, and Thailand. They are very easy to grow, even in cooler regions (although the flavor will be less intense). Even a few plants will reward the grower with a crop of delicious chiles, which can either be used immediately or frozen.

As this collection of recipes proves, chiles can be used in appetizers, soups and main dishes of very type. They make marvelous sauces, relishes, and pickles. It is worth getting to know at least a handful of the different varieties, for each has its own distinctive flavor.

Used fresh, chiles add flavor or fire to salads and salsas; broiled and skinned, they have a smoky taste that is so good that they are often served solo, streaked with olive oil; pounded or puréed, they make their presence felt in sauces and stews. In a stir-fry they can play a starring role or simply supply a subtle undertone.

Not surprisingly, chiles have a particular affinity for bell peppers, and are often broiled alongside these, their less flamboyant cousins. The combination works particularly well in vegetarian dishes, which can often be somewhat bland.

Handle chiles cautiously: they contain capsaicin, an ingredient which can cause irritation to tender skin, and considerable discomfort if it comes into contact with the nose or eyes. Capsaicin is not removed by water, so always wash your hands very thoroughly with soap after handling chiles or – better still – wear gloves. Thin surgical gloves are particularly useful.

If you are wary about chiles, use them sparingly at first, remembering that as a general rule unripe (green) chiles are cooler than ripe red ones, and that most of the fire resides in the membrane and seeds. Experiment with different varieties: Anaheims, for instance, are milder than jalapeños, which in turn generate less heat than habaneros.

Get to know the varieties of dried chile, too. With a selection of these in your store cupboard, together with canned chiles, hot pepper sauces, pastes, and powders, you'll have a fine range of flavorings at your fingertips.

A GLOBAL GUIDE TO FRESH AND DRIED CHILES

WHEN BUYING FRESH chiles, look for specimens that are firm, shiny, dry, and heavy, with a fresh clean aroma; avoid those that are discolored or limp. Rinse and dry, then wrap in paper towels and store in the salad compartment of the refrigerator, where they will keep for 2 to 3 weeks. If chiles are kept in plastic bags, moisture will build up and they will spoil; if not kept in the refrigerator, they will quickly shrivel and become limp.

Remember that the heat is in the membrane or vein, as well as the seeds, so when a recipe calls for the chile to be seeded, the membrane needs to be removed as well. If a hotter flavor is required than the chile you are using will provide, simply leave the seeds and membrane intact. It is worth noting that everyone's heat tolerance varies, and what one person finds hot, another will not. It is also true to say that tolerance to the heat of chiles can be acquired. The more chiles you eat, the more you will be able to eat with enjoyment. In Mexico it is not unusual to see children chomping on chiles as if they were cherries.

Once you have become accustomed to chiles, it is well worth experimenting by combining two or three varieties in the same dish, thus imparting a different flavor. The jalapeño is the most widely available chile in the United States, but a chile-lover is likely to scoff at the ordinariness of the jalapeño, favoring a serrano, a habanero, or a Thai bird's eye chile instead. An amateur may brag about how hot he likes his chiles, but a true connoisseur will talk about the underlying flavors – the earthy, slightly chocolate flavor of the poblano, the hot-sweet intensity of a cayenne, the fiery fruit flavor of a habanero.

DRIED CHILES

Like wine, dried chiles have many different flavors and it takes a connoisseur to detect the subtle differences. They vary from rich smoky and woody flavors to fruity flavors redolent of cherries, plums or damsons, those that have a distinct citrus flavor and even some with a chocolate, licorice or coffee flavor. It takes time to develop the palate by learning about the different flavors, but it is time well spent. Chiles can transport an ordinary dish to new culinary heights, as their depth and richness in flavor is incomparable. The drying process intensifies the flavor and gives it a real punch. On drying, the natural sugars concentrate and produce the great depth of flavors that are present.

When buying dried chiles, check that they have no discoloration or spots and are clean, not dirty or dusty. If the chile is split, much of its oil will have been lost, resulting in an inferior taste. Store in an airtight container for 3 to 4 months, certainly no longer than 6 months.

As with fresh chiles, there are many different varieties of dried chiles and if one is not available, another, or even chili powder, can be substituted. If powder is used, the flavor will, however, not be as good. Any fresh chile can be dried but the more obscure varieties are difficult to find outside their country of origin.

MIX AND MATCH

If a particular type of chile is specified in a recipe and is unobtainable, either substitute one of the equivalent heat or use more chiles with a lower heat content.

ANAHEIM – Heat 2–3

The Anaheim, also called the California chile, is 5 to 7 inches long and 1 inch or so wide. The mildest member of the chile family, it is a cousin of the New Mexico chile.

The Anaheim is widely available fresh, probably second to the jalapeño, and is often canned and labeled simply "green chiles." It is pale green, ripening to red and has fairly thick smooth skin. Dried, it is a deep burgundy color and is one of the most readily available dried chiles. A mild California chili powder is made from the Anaheim. When Anaheims are used in the making of dishes like Chili con Carne, hotter chiles are usually added.

ANCHO – Heat 3–5

The Ancho is actually a dried poblano chile. It is readily available. Before drying, the chile is ripened and has a deep reddish brown, wrinkled skin. Not to be confused with the mulato, which has a blackish tinge to the skin and is neither as sharp nor as fruity as the ancho. About 5 inches in length, the chile has a sweet fruit flavor with hints of raisin, coffee, and licorice. The ancho, mulato, and pasilla form the holy trinity of chiles, and are used to make the traditional Mexican mole dishes and sauces.

ARBOL – Heat 8

The *chile de arbol* is narrow, about 3 inches long, and bright orange-red. It is very hot. It is most often found dried – sometimes labeled only "dried red chiles" – although other small, hot, dried red chiles such as serranos may also be labeled as *chiles de arbol*. Pure *chile de arbol* powder may be found in the Mexican section of some very well-stocked grocery stores.

BANANA CHILE – Heat 2–3

About 6 inches in length, the banana chile ranges in color from pale green to light orange. It has a sweet flavor similar to a bell pepper, and thick flesh. The inside of the flesh is often rubbed with chili powder to impart a stronger flavor. Banana chiles are ideal for stuffing and salads.

CAYENNE – Heat 8

The cayenne is bright red, thin, and pointed, 3 to 7 inches long. It is extremely hot, yet sweet, with a flavor that resembles that of Thai bird's eye chiles, and is an ingredient in Asian as well as Mexican dishes. It is most familiar dried and ground into cayenne pepper – sometimes called simply red pepper – which will add heat but not much flavor to any dish.

CHIPOTLE – Heat 6

A large dried smoked jalapeño, this is dull tan to coffee brown, about 2 to 4 inches in length. Often available in cans or jars, these chiles are hot and are normally used with their seeds and membranes intact. The *chipotle grande* is a dried huachinango chile which is similar in flavor but larger in size.

CONGO – Heat 8

As the name suggests this chile comes from the Congo. It is also grown in Mombasa and Zanzibar. A small, green, very hot chile which turns red on ripening, it is ¼ to ½ inch in length.

DE AGUA – Heat 4–5

About 4½ inches in length, tapering to a point, the chile may be green or red, both having a vegetable flavor similar to unripe tomatoes with a thin flesh. The red has a slightly sweeter flavor. Grown in South America. Ideal for soups, mole sauces and stuffing.

DUTCH – Heat 6

Also known as Holland chile, this bright red chile is slightly curved, about 4 inches in length. It has a hot sweet flavor and thick flesh. The Thai chile or red fresno can be substituted. Grown in the Netherlands, it is ideal for soups, casseroles, sauces and pickling.

FRESNO – Heat 6–7

Either green or red, about 2 inches in length, the fresno is full and plump, tapering to a round end. It has a thick flesh and is sweet and hot. Ideal for salsas, stuffing and sauces.

GUAJILLO – Heat 2–4

One of the most-common dried chiles available, the guajillo is about 4 to 6 inches in length with a rough maroon skin. It has a slightly bitter or tannin flavor and the skin is often discarded after rehydration due to its toughness.

HABANERO – Heat 10

One of the two hottest chiles in the world, the habanero – its name means from Havana – is most widely used in the Yucatan, but has recently gained popularity among masochists in the U.S. The habanero is lantern shaped and looks like a miniature bell pepper, just 2 inches high. Its color ranges from green to bright orange. When ripe, it is sweet, with a tropical fruit flavor. It is related to the Scotch Bonnet, an equally hot chile from the Caribbean. Fresh habaneros are showing up in a growing number of well-stocked grocery stores, especially those in Hispanic or Caribbean neighborhoods. Habanero chili powder and crushed dried habaneros are scarce but can be found.

HONKA OR HONTAKA – Heat 9

From ¾ to 3 inches in length, this orange or red chile from Japan has a wrinkled appearance.

HUNGARIAN CHERRY PEPPER – Heat 1–3

This round chile is about 1½ inches in diameter. Bright red, it has plump flesh and masses of seeds and is sweet in flavor and fairly mild in heat. Hungarian cherry peppers are grown in Hungary, Europe, and California. They are ideal for salads.

HUNGARIAN SWEET CHILE – Heat 0–1

About 6 inches in length, this sweet chile is broad at the stem with a rounded end. Bright red, mild in heat with a thick flesh, they taste very like the bell peppers when used as pimientos. Grown in Hungary, Europe, and California, they are ideal for any dish where heat is not a requirement.

JALAPEÑO – Heat 5–6

The jalapeño, the most widely available fresh chile in the U.S., is hot, although there are many varieties of chile that are hotter. Smooth, glossy jalapeños are usually 2 to 3 inches long, tapering to a rounded end. Although most are sold green, they will turn bright red if left on the bush to ripen. Several raw, chopped, and unseeded jalapeños added to chili will turn up the heat considerably. Roasting jalapeños gives them a marvelous flavor, but they do not need to be roasted. Dried jalapeños are quite scarce. Jalapeño chili powder is also hard to find. Smoked jalapeños, called *chipotles*, have a wonderful, not at all subtle, smoky flavor. They do not lose any of

their heat in the smoking process. Chipotles are available canned in adobo sauce, and can occasionally be found dried. Tart, pickled jalapeños, called *jalapeños en escabeche*, are more often used as a garnish than a main ingredient.

JAMAICAN HOT – Heat 9

These are about 2 inches in length, bright red and similar in shape to the Scotch Bonnet or habanero, to which they are related. The flesh is thin, with a sweet, hot flavor. Grown in Jamaica and other Caribbean islands, these hot chiles are ideal for curries, fish stews and chutneys.

KALYANPUR, KESANAKURRU AND KOVILPATT – Heat varies

These are all Indian chiles that are used extensively throughout the country. Green and red.

KASHMIR – Heat 6–8

Closely related to the jalapeño and serrano chiles, they are green or red, about 1 to 2 inches in length. Also called sriracha or siracha. A sauce is made from these chiles in Thailand and sold around the world as an accompaniment to fish.

KENYAN – Heat 2–3

About 1 to 2 inches in length, the Kenyan chile looks like a jalapeño. Often sold when bright green, the chile turns red when ripe. Grown in Kenya and surrounding countries.

KOREAN – Heat 6–7

Related to the Thai or bird's eye chile, this is about 3 to 4 inches in length, thin and slightly curved, tapering to a point. Bright green and thin-fleshed, the chile has a hot vegetable flavor. Grown in Korea, Japan, and California, it is ideal for stir-fries, marinades, chutneys and pickling.

MULATO – Heat 3

About 5 inches in length, this dried chile is dark brown. Round at the stem, it tapers to a point. It has a smokier flavor than the ancho and the predominant taste is licorice with a hint of tobacco and cherry. Like the ancho, it is sold in Mexico in three different grades, varying in depth or taste and quality.

NEW MEXICO – Heat 3–4

This is the chile that Southwesterners rhapsodize about. The New Mexico chile is a relative of the Anaheim and resembles it in size and shape, but inspires far more passion than its Californian cousin. It is a light to medium green and darkens to a deep red if left on the bush to ripen. These chiles freeze extremely well. They are ideal for salsas, sauces, stuffing, and casseroles; the red chiles are also used in red chili and barbecue sauces. New Mexico chili powders are also popular.

PASILLA – Heat 4

Also called the *chile negro,* the pasilla is very dark, purple-black in color.

It is long and slim like the Anaheim, but has wrinkled skin. The flavor is intense and moderately spicy, with just a bit more heat and none of the sweetness of the poblano. It is more readily available dried than fresh, and is often used in commercial chili powder blends. The dried poblano is sometimes mislabeled as pasilla. Held up to the light, a dried poblano (called an *ancho*) is reddish, while the pasilla is brown-black.

POBLANO – Heat 3

Green or red, this thick-fleshed chile is 4 to 5 inches in length. Although only a moderately spicy chile, the poblano has a complex, earthy flavor with hints of chocolate. Green chili stews are usually made with poblanos, which can be used in the large quantities required without making the stew scorchingly hot. In a hot chili, poblanos are used in combination with hotter chiles. The poblano is almost always roasted and peeled. Strips of roasted poblanos, called rajas, make delicious garnishes for chili.

PRIK CHEE FA – Heat 5–8

A very popular Thai chile, "prik" being the Thai name for chile. A red chile about 4 inches in length and fat in shape.

SANTAKA – Heat 9

A very straight, thin, deep red chile, the santaka is grown in Japan.

SCOTCH BONNET – Heat 10

The incendiary Scotch Bonnet is a relative of the habanero and is often confused with its equally fiery cousin. The Scotch Bonnet is about an inch in length and looks like a tiny tam-o'-shanter in colors of green, yellow, orange, and red. Grown in Jamaica and other Caribbean islands, it is not widely available in the U.S., but a diligent search may find it in a grocery in a West Indian neighborhood.

SERRANO – Heat 7

Small – about 2 inches long – and thin, the serrano is hotter than the jalapeño but not as hot as the cayenne or habanero. The flavor has been described as clean and biting. It is usually sold when glossy green, but it turns red if left on the bush. It can be substituted for the Thai or bird's eye chile in the ratio of 3 serrano chiles to 1 Thai chile. Serranos are ideal for guacamole, stir-fries, and salsas.

TABASCO – Heat 9

About 1 inch in length, thin-fleshed with a strong, biting heat. Bright orange or red and used mainly for making the famous Tabasco sauce. Grown in Louisiana and Central and South America.

THAI OR BIRD'S EYE – Heat 7–8

About 1½ inches in length, this is a thin elongated green or red chile with a pointed end. Thin-fleshed with many seeds, it has a fierce heat. Grown in Thailand, Asia and California, these chiles are ideal for stir-fries and all Asian dishes.

POWDERS, PASTES AND SAUCES

Most dried chiles can be ground successfully, and in parts of the world where the chile is king, it is not uncommon to see powders made from a specific type of chile. In the United States, chili powder is a mixture of spices and herbs. It usually includes pure ground chiles, cumin, oregano, and garlic powder, but each manufacturer has an individual blend. Typically ancho or pasilla chili powder is used. Onion, allspice, and salt may also be added. The powder provides an underlying chile flavor but not much heat. When it is used for making Chili con Carne, cayenne, or Tabasco sauce, crushed chili flakes or a pure chili powder are usually added.

Some spice companies also produce a more fiery blend, called hot or Mexican chili powder, which will add moderate heat to a dish. Across the Atlantic, chili powder usually means the pure product: dried chiles that have been coarsely ground. British chili powder is more pungent than the darker American product.

When buying chili powder, look for a product with a deep rich color. It should neither be too powdery nor too dry; the best consistency is slightly lumpy, indicating that the natural oils have not been lost. These oils should leave a slight stain on the fingers when rubbed, and the aroma should be intense.

CAYENNE
Made from a single variety of chile and often referred to as cayenne pepper, this is a pungent, finely ground deep-colored spice.

KOREAN CHILI POWDER
Regarded as one of the finest chili powders in the world, this is a relatively mild, coarse powder which tastes like a cross between paprika and cayenne. It has a glowing carmine color.

PAPRIKA
Ranging from mild and sweet to warm and pungent – but never hot – paprika is widely used in Hungarian cooking. It has a slightly bitter aftertaste. The color varies from rose through to deep scarlet. Like all ground spices, paprika is best used as soon as possible after opening. Some cooks recommend storing it in the refrigerator.

RED PEPPER
Made from pungent but not particularly potent chiles, this spice comes from Turkey. The flavor is sometimes enhanced by roasting. Red Pepper is also the name sometimes given to cayenne.

CHILI FLAKES
Also called *chile caribe*, these are crushed, dried red chiles, usually New Mexico chiles, and are almost always hot. They are often used to give heat to sauces, pickles, and sausages.

MAKING YOUR OWN CHILI POWDER
Preheat the oven to 400°F. Select one variety of dried chile or a mixture. Spread out the chiles on an ungreased baking sheet and roast them for a few minutes, until they are somewhat brittle and fragrant. Do not let them darken or they will have an unpleasant burnt flavor. Let the chiles cool, then remove the stems and seeds, cut or crumble them into pieces and place them in a mortar. Grind with a pestle until fine, or use a food processor or spice grinder.

PASTES AND SAUCES

CHILI PASTE

A thick purée, which varies in intensity, this is sometimes available from specialist delis, either on its own or as an ingredient in a sauce.

SAUCES AND OILS

SAUCES

There are a number of well-known chili – or hot pepper – sauces, including the famous Tabasco. This is made from the fermented Tabasco chile, with vinegar and salt. The Tabasco chile, a cousin of the cayenne, comes from the Mexican state of the same name. It is a small, red, fiery chile that is not available commercially. Tabasco sauce has been produced since before the Civil War, but as the world's taste for chiles and spicy foods has developed, it has had competition from a great variety of hot pepper sauces.

These include the hot pepper sauces of the West Indies, which are generally based upon the devishly hot habaneros, also known as country peppers or bird peppers (this last because even the birds in the islands have developed a taste for fiery cuisine, and nibble on them). Habaneros rank amongst the hottest peppers in the world. Sauces in the Caribbean give some indication of this: their names include *Jamaica Hellfire*, *Hell In A Bottle* and *Melinda's XXXtra Hot Sauce*.

OILS

The most familiar chili oil is a Chinese product, made by heating dried red chiles and vegetable oil together. Many cooks also make their own chili oil by the simple expedient of steeping dried red chiles in oil. The result not only looks attractive, but creates a flavorsome oil for cooking or using in salad dressings. The intensity can be varied by the amount of chiles used, and some cooks add bruised garlic cloves as well.

JERK SEASONING

This is a Caribbean product which originated centuries ago, when the Arawak Indians preserved meat by rubbing strips of it with a mixture of spices and acidic chiles before cooking it slowly over an aromatic wood fire until it was bone dry but still flavorful. The preservation technique was adopted by escaped African slaves in Jamaica to provide food for when they were on the run. Drying of meat in this way was nothing new – native American Indians used the technique and it was also known in Africa – but the jerk spice mixes (so called because the dried meat was known as jerky) became a Caribbean specialty. Soon the technique was extended to the cooking of fresh meat, and steaks and hams were rubbed with a combination of spices and chiles, with additional ingredients, before being chargrilled or smoked. Families

guarded their jerk seasoning recipes jealously. Some added lime juice or vinegar; others sweetened the mixture with sugar or molasses. Jerk seasonings and sauces remain very popular today, and are sold commercially.

OTHER PRODUCTS

Canned chiles are also available but it is generally preferable to use fresh or dried chiles. Large canned chiles can be stuffed, and pickled jalapeños (*en escabeche*) are useful.

USING CHILES

ROASTING FRESH CHILES
STEP 1

Remove freshly roasted chiles from the broiler.

STEP 2

Place chiles in a plastic bag to cool.

STEP 3

Peel off the skins

REMOVING THE SEEDS
If a recipe recommends seeding a chile, cut off the stem end, split the pod open and scrape out the seeds and membrane with a teaspoon. Rinse and gently pat dry with paper towels.

ROASTING FRESH CHILES
Roasting fresh chiles gives them a wonderful flavor and takes the edge off their heat. It also allows easy removal of the tough skin on some larger chiles, such as Anaheims and poblanos. Smaller chiles, including habaneros, serranos, and jalapeños, do not need to have their thin skins removed, but may be roasted for improved flavor.

Place the chiles – whole or in two or three large pieces – under a preheated broiler. Cook for a few minutes, turning frequently, until the skin blisters and blackens. Take care, however, not to burn the flesh. You can also grip each chile in turn with tongs and hold it over a gas flame to blister, or dip it quickly into hot oil. Once the chiles have blistered, place them in a bowl and cover with several paper towels, or put them in a plastic bag. Leave them to cool, then peel off the skins or rub them off under cold running water, if necessary. Remove the membranes and seeds if you like.

DRYING CHILES
Mature fresh chiles can easily be dried. Simply thread them on heavy cotton thread. Use a needle with a large eye and pierce each chile just below the stem. Hang the chiles in a warm, dry place for about a week. A whole dried chile, added to a casserole, will give just a hint of heat, and can be removed at the end of cooking. Dried chiles can also be ground.

DRY ROASTING DRIED CHILES
The flavor of large dried chiles will be improved if they are dry roasted before being used. Heat a nonstick skillet, add the chiles and sear them for 2 to 3 minutes, or until they begin to soften and grow plump. On no account allow them to burn or the flavor will be ruined.

REHYDRATING DRIED CHILES
To rehydrate dried chiles, remove the stems and seeds and cut each chile into two or three pieces. Put them in a deep,

narrow heatproof bowl. Pour in very hot (but not boiling) water to cover. Stir, make sure all the pieces are immersed in water, then let stand for 30 minutes. Pour the chiles and their soaking water into a blender or food processor. Whiz until smooth, then press through a strainer. Use the strained sauce in cooking. The chiles can also be simmered in water, beer or stock before being puréed.

GARNISHING WITH CHILES

Brightly colored chiles make a wonderful garnish. Tie a bunch of them with raffia or colored twine to garnish a large platter of food that features them, or carve one or two into chile flowers. To do this, choose perfect chiles with smooth, unmarked skins. Rinse each chile lightly and pat dry with paper towels. Holding a chile by the stem, slit it in half lengthwise. Scrape out the seeds. Keeping the stem intact, cut the chile lengthwise into strips or petals. Put the chile in a bowl of ice water and repeat the process with the remaining chiles. Leave for 10 minutes, until the chile petals have curled to form flowers. Drain the chiles, dry lightly and use as a decorative garnish.

Chopped or sliced chiles also make a good garnish, as do pickled jalapeños. Simply scatter them over the finished dish to add color and extra piquancy.

SAFETY FIRST

It is essential to handle chiles carefully: the unwise cook who carelessly rubs his or her eye after chopping chiles is in for considerable pain. The culprit is capsaicin, the oily substance which gives them their fiery nature. Capsaicin does not dissolve in water, so it is important to soap your hands thoroughly after working with chiles.

Wearing latex gloves is the ideal answer, but this will not prevent capsaicin from getting onto knives, chopping boards and other utensils. Wash these thoroughly, preferably in the dishwasher.

If you do have the misfortune to touch delicate skin after handling chiles, rubbing the stinging spot with a little shortening may help. Burning lips, tongue or throat can be eased by a swallow of milk, sour cream or yogurt. Avoid drinking water, which will not help and may even make the problem worse.

DIPS & SNACKS

GUACAMOLE

Serves 4

The cool appearance of this delicious dip is deceptive: contrasting with the creamy avocado is the fiery flavor of chile.
Guacamole is great for parties. Serve it with carrot and celery sticks and traditional taco chips.

INGREDIENTS

2 ripe avocados

1½ cups peeled, seeded, and finely chopped ripe tomatoes

1 bunch scallions, trimmed and finely chopped

2 serrano chiles, seeded and finely chopped

1 or 2 jalapeño chiles, seeded and finely chopped

2 tbsp lime juice

1½ tbsp freshly chopped cilantro

salt and pepper

shredded lime peel, for the garnish

taco chips and crudités, to serve

Peel the avocados and discard the seeds. Mash the flesh with a potato masher or fork.

Add the finely chopped tomato and scallions with the chiles and mix together well. Stir in the lime juice with the cilantro and seasoning to taste. Spoon into a bowl and fork the top.

Sprinkle with the lime peel just before serving with taco chips and crudités. Guacamole is best eaten immediately but if it has to be kept, place one of the avocado seeds in the middle, cover and chill for no longer than 1 hour.

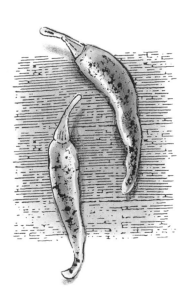

THAI HORS D'OEUVRE

Serves 6 to 8

This colorful selection of ingredients on a leaf-strewn platter is a tempting invitation for guests to make their own flavorsome lettuce parcels.

INGREDIENTS

5 tbsp unsweetened grated coconut, roasted at 350°F until light brown

3 tbsp finely diced shallots

3 tbsp finely diced lime

3 tbsp diced gingerroot or candied ginger

3 tbsp chopped dried baby shrimp

3 tbsp unsalted roasted peanuts

2 tsp chopped fresh small green Thai chiles

vine or other edible leaves, for decorating platter

lettuce leaves, for serving

SAUCE

2 tbsp unsweetened coconut

½ tbsp shrimp paste

1½ tsp sliced gingerroot

½ tsp sliced shallot

3 tbsp chopped unsalted peanuts

2 tbsp chopped dried baby shrimp

1 cup palm sugar or dark brown sugar

2½ cups water

First make the sauce: roast the shredded coconut with the shrimp paste, gingerroot, and shallot in a 350°F oven for 5 minutes until fragrant, then let cool. Place the peanuts and shrimp in a blender or food processor and chop finely, or pound with a mortar and pestle.

Pour the mixture into a heavy pan. Add the sugar and water. Mix well and bring to a boil then lower the heat and simmer until the sauce is reduced

to about 1¼ cups. Remove from the heat and let cool.

To serve, pour the sauce into a serving bowl and arrange all the ingredients in separate piles on a platter or in small bowls. Have the lettuce leaves ready in a separate bowl. To eat, take a lettuce leaf, place a small amount of each of the garnishes in the middle, top with a spoonful of sauce and fold up into a little package.

CHILE CON QUESO

Serves 8 to 12

Chile con queso is a sort of Southwestern fondue-melted cheese with chiles, onions, garlic, and tomatoes. It is a terrific dip for chips, crackers, or crudités, or can be a main dish fondue, served with chunks of bread. It can be kept warm by setting the pot over a candle or on a warming tray. For a mild dip, remove the seeds and veins from the jalapeños.

INGREDIENTS

2 tbsp butter

2 or 3 jalapeño chiles, minced

1 garlic clove, minced

1 medium tomato, seeded and chopped

3 green onions, minced

2 cups grated Cheddar cheese

2 cups grated Monterey Jack cheese

Preheat the oven to 350°F.

Heat the butter in a skillet and sauté the chiles, garlic, tomatoes, and green onions for 5 minutes. Continue cooking, if needed, until the liquids have evaporated.

Stir the vegetables into the shredded cheese in an ovenproof serving dish. Bake until the cheese is bubbling, about 12 minutes. Serve immediately while piping hot.

BEAN DIP WITH CHILE

Serves 6 to 8

INGREDIENTS

3 or 4 jalapeño chiles

2 tsp corn or olive oil

1⅓ cups drained and rinsed canned red kidney beans

1⅓ cups drained and rinsed canned cannellini beans

1 or 2 garlic cloves, minced

4 to 5 tbsp tomato juice

1 ripe mango, peeled and sliced

1 tbsp freshly chopped oregano

extra freshly chopped oregano, for the garnish

crudités, for serving

Preheat the broiler to high. Place the chiles in a broiler pan and drizzle with the oil. Broil for 4 to 5 minutes, or until the skins have blistered and blackened.

Put the chiles into a plastic bag and leave to sweat for 10 minutes; then discard the skin and seeds if a milder dip is required. Put into a food processor with the remaining ingredients and blend to form a thick dipping consistency.

Pour into a serving dish, cover and chill for 30 minutes to allow the flavors to develop. Sprinkle with chopped oregano, and serve with the crudités.

▶ *Chile con Queso*

SPICED EGGPLANT PURÉE

Serves 6

Baked eggplant, puréed with chiles and spices, makes a marvelous, creamy dip. Cumin seeds add crunch.

INGREDIENTS

2 large eggplants, about 1 lb in weight

4 red Anaheim chiles

4 garlic cloves

grated peel and juice of 1 large lemon

1 tsp ground cumin

1 tsp ground coriander

1 tsp ground cinnamon

¾ cup cream cheese

cumin seeds for the garnish

pita breads and crudités, for serving

Preheat the oven to 400°F. Rinse the eggplant and prick each of them a few times. Place directly on an oven shelf in the oven and bake for 40 minutes, or until the eggplant are very soft and have begun to collapse. Put the chiles and garlic on a baking sheet and place on another shelf. Cook the chiles and garlic for about 10 minutes, or until the skins have begun to wrinkle. Remove from the oven and put into a plastic bag for 10 minutes. Peel and discard the seeds from the chiles and the skins from the garlic, and set aside.

Let the eggplant cool, then strip off the skin and put the flesh into a food processor with the chiles, garlic, lemon peel and juice. Add the spices. Process to a smooth purée, then add the cream cheese and process again. Transfer to a serving bowl and fork the top.

Chill for at least 30 minutes. Garnish with the cumin seeds and serve with pita breads and crudités.

HOT AND SMOKY FISH PÂTÉ

Serves 6 to 8

You can use any smoked fish for this tangy pâté. Serve with an assortment of crackers. The pâté also tastes good spooned onto celery sticks or as a topping for fingers of toast.

INGREDIENTS

1 lb smoked marlin

½ cup sweet pickle relish

¼ cup prepared horseradish sauce

1 small onion, chopped

1 celery stalk, finely chopped

1 mild red chile, seeded and chopped

½ tsp lime juice

1 tsp hot pepper sauce

⅓ cup mayonnaise

salt and pepper

Chop the fish coarsely and place it in a mixing bowl. Add the relish, horseradish, onion, celery, chile, and lime juice, and mix well. Add half the hot pepper sauce and half the mayonnaise. Mix well and taste. Add more hot sauce, according to your taste. Stir in more mayonnaise and mix until the desired texture and flavor is achieved.

CHALUPAS

Serves 4

Tortillas form the basis of many Mexican dishes such as enchiladas, burritos, and empanadas. They are often filled with a variety of savory mixtures and almost always served with a side dish of refried beans.

INGREDIENTS

TORTILLAS

2½ cups all-purpose flour

1 tsp salt

1 tsp baking powder

1 tbsp lard or shortening

¾ cup water

SAUCE

2 tsp sunflower oil

1 small onion, chopped

2 red jalapeño chiles, seeded and chopped

14-oz can crushed tomatoes

FILLING

½ small iceberg lettuce, shredded

1 cup Refried Beans (page 26)

½ cup grated hard cheese, such as Cheddar

4 scallions, trimmed and chopped

2 red jalapeño chiles, seeded and chopped

sour cream and lime wedges, for serving

Make the tortillas by mixing the flour, salt, and baking powder in a bowl, cutting in the lard or shortening and adding enough of the water to make a stiff dough. Divide the dough into eight pieces and shape into small balls.

Use a tortilla press, if you have one, to make eight tortillas. Alternatively, place each ball of dough in turn between two plastic bags and roll out to a thin round, 6 inches across.

Heat a heavy nonstick skillet and cook each tortilla for about 2 minutes on each side, or until the edges begin to lift and the surfaces are lightly browned. Wrap the cooked tortillas in paper towels and foil so that they stay hot while you cook the chili sauce.

Heat the oil in a small pan and gently sauté the onion and chiles for 5 minutes. Stir in the crushed tomatoes and bring to a boil. Reduce the heat and simmer for 15 minutes. Let cool slightly, then press through a strainer to form a smooth purée. Cover and keep warm.

Warm, the tortillas if necessary by placing in a nonstick skillet for about 30 seconds. Dampen the edges, then shape and pinch up the sides of each to form a boat shape.

Fill the tortillas with the shredded lettuce and place the refried beans on top. Spoon a little of the prepared sauce over. Divide the cheese among the tortillas and sprinkle over the scallions and chopped chiles. Serve with sour cream and lime wedges.

COOK'S TIP

The best way to reheat tortillas is over a direct flame. Pat them with damp hands if they are uncomfortably dry. Alternatively, wrap them in a clean dish towel or napkin and reheat them in the microwave on High for 40 to 50 seconds, or wrap foil around the cloth package and reheat them in a low oven. If you use bought tortillas, or taco shells, reheat them as directed on the package.

QUESADILLAS WITH REFRIED BEANS

Serves 4

Quesadillas usually consist of tortillas filled with cheese, folded in half and cooked until the cheese melts. In this snack version, the tortillas are simply sandwiched together with melted cheese, cut in quarters and served with the ever-popular refried beans.

INGREDIENTS

8 freshly cooked wheat tortillas (page 24)

2 cups grated hard cheese

sliced red chiles, dill pickles, 1 lime slice and 1 stuffed green olive, for the garnish

REFRIED BEANS

2 cups pinto or black beans, picked over and soaked overnight

3 onions, chopped

5 or 10 garlic cloves, chopped

2 serrano chiles, sliced

10 oz bacon, diced

salt

3 tbsp vegetable oil

½ tsp ground cumin

½ tsp mild chili powder

COOK'S TIP
Refried beans are traditionally cooked in a generous amount of lard. This version is lower in fat. To save time you could use canned refried beans.

Make the refried beans. Drain the beans, place them in a large saucepan and add water to cover. Bring to a boil and cook for 1 minute, then remove from the heat and let stand, covered, for 1 hour.

Add half the onions to the beans, with the garlic, chiles, and bacon. Pour over water to cover and bring to a boil again. Reduce the heat and simmer for 1½ to 2 hours, until the beans are softened. Drain off any excess liquid, then mash or purée the bean mixture to a chunky consistency. Add salt to taste.

Heat the oil in a large skillet and sauté the remaining onion until soft. Sprinkle in the cumin and chili powder,

cook for 1 minute, then ladle in a scoop of the bean mixture. Cook over medium-high heat until thick and darkened in color, then add another scoop of beans. Repeat until all the beans have simmered to a thick flavorful mixture. Check the seasoning and add more salt if needed.

Sprinkle the cheese over half the soft, freshly cooked tortillas, and place the remaining tortillas on top. Heat the tortilla "sandwiches" in a heavy nonstick skillet until the cheese has melted, then cut them in quarters and serve with the refried beans. Garnish with the chiles, dill pickles, lime slices, and olive.

SPICY PEPPER PIZZA

Serves 4

Chiles and mixed peppers make for a colorful pizza topping with plenty of flavor. Add sliced pepperoni if you like.

INGREDIENTS

1 tbsp sunflower oil

1 onion chopped

2 garlic cloves, crushed

5 red jalapeño chiles, seeded and thinly sliced

14-oz can crushed tomatoes

2 tbsp tomato paste

2 tbsp freshly chopped oregano

2 tsp ground cumin

2 prepared 8-inch pizza bases

2 red bell peppers, skinned and seeded

2 green bell peppers, skinned and seeded

2 yellow bell peppers, skinned and seeded

1½ cups grated mozzarella cheese

⅓ cup pitted black olives

Preheat oven to 400°F. Lightly oil two baking sheets.

Heat the oil in a pan and sauté the onion, garlic and chiles for 5 minutes. Add the crushed tomatoes, tomato paste, oregano, and cumin, and bring to a boil. Reduce the heat and simmer for 10 to 15 minutes, or until the mixture forms a thick sauce.

Spread the sauce over the pizza bases. Slice the peppers and arrange on top of the sauce. Cover with the cheese and arrange the olives on top. Bake for 25 minutes, or until the cheese is golden and bubbly.

VEGETARIAN ENCHILADAS

Serves 4

Tortillas are delicious with a spicy vegetable filling. Vary the vegetables to suit the season. If you keep a pack of ready-to-use wheat tortillas in the storecupboard, this makes a quick and easy snack.

INGREDIENTS

2 tbsp sunflower oil

1 large onion, thinly sliced

2 garlic cloves, crushed

4 green de agua chiles, seeded and sliced

2¼ cups peeled, seeded and chopped ripe tomatoes

1 tbsp tomato paste mixed with 1 tbsp water

2 zucchini, trimmed and cut into matchsticks

1½ cups grated hard cheese, such as Cheddar

6 scallions, trimmed and chopped

8 freshly cooked wheat tortillas (page 24)

fresh herbs, for the garnish

Chile Pepper Relish (below) to serve

Preheat the oven to 400°F. Heat the oil in a skillet and gently sauté the onion, garlic, and chiles for 5 minutes. Add the tomatoes and the tomato paste mixture and bring to a boil. Cover the pan, reduce the heat and simmer for 15 minutes.

Stir in the zucchini, 1 cup of the cheese and the scallions.

Divide the filling among the tortillas and fold them into quarters. Place in a shallow baking dish and sprinkle with the remaining cheese. Bake for 15 minutes, or until the cheese is golden and bubbly. Garnish with herbs and serve immediately while hot with the Chile Pepper Relish.

CHILE PEPPER RELISH

Makes about 1¼ cups

This can also be served as an appetizer with crudités and taco chips.

INGREDIENTS

1½ cups peeled, seeded and chopped ripe tomatoes

2 shallots, finely chopped

2 or 3 red serrano chiles, seeded and chopped

1 garlic clove, crushed

1 tsp salt

3 tbsp freshly chopped cilantro

1 tbsp lime juice or cider vinegar

3-inch piece cucumber, peeled and finely chopped

1 tbsp pumpkin seeds, roasted and then finely ground

cilantro sprigs, for the garnish

Put the tomatoes into a bowl and stir in the shallots, chiles, garlic, salt, cilantro, and lime juice or vinegar. Mix together well, then cover and leave for at least 30 minutes to let the flavors develop.

Stir in the cucumber and pumpkin seeds. Garnish with the cilantro sprigs.

▶ *Vegetarian Enchiladas*

EMPANADAS

Serves 4

Empanadas are little turnovers that may contain sweet or savory ingredients. As so often, you can use both your imagination and leftovers to the full; this is a basic savory empanada.

INGREDIENTS

2 tbsp olive oil

1 medium onion, finely chopped

1 small red or green bell pepper, seeded and chopped

2 medium tomatoes skinned, seeded and chopped

8 oz ground beef

1 dried red chile (arbol or similar)

½ tsp cumin seed

1 tablespoon golden raisins

salt and pepper

1 lb prepared piecrust dough

Preheat the oven to 375°F. Heat the oil in a skillet and sauté the onion, pepper, and tomatoes until soft. Add the ground beef and fry until the meat is brown and crumbly.

Crumble in the dried chile. Use the cumin seeds whole, or for better flavor, crush them using a pestle and mortar. Add the cumin and raisins to the mixture in the skillet. Season to taste, and cook for another 10 minutes or so. Let cool.

Roll the dough into eight 5-inch rounds. Divide the filling equally among them, placing it on one half of the round and folding over to seal. Overfilling will make cooking difficult!

Place on a baking sheet and bake for about 35 minutes, until the empanadas are golden brown. Serve hot. Some people prefer to deep-fry their empanadas.

SPICY POTATO PATTIES

Serves 4

Hot chiles and cool mint gives these potato patties a superb flavor.

INGREDIENTS

2 large potatoes (about 14 oz) diced

1 tbsp freshly chopped mint

1 tbsp lemon juice

½ tsp salt

1 small onion, finely chopped

2 tsp coriander seeds, crushed

1 tsp cumin seeds

¼ tsp chile powder

2 green chiles, finely chopped

3 tbsp freshly chopped cilantro

1 egg

salt and pepper

2 tsp oil

Cook the potatoes in boiling salted water until they are tender.

Meanwhile, mix the lemon juice, mint, and a pinch of salt with the onion in a bowl. Set this mixture for filling the patties to one side.

Drain the potatoes and mash them lightly so that the mixture is still slightly lumpy. Add the coriander and cumin seeds, with the chili powder, green chiles, cilantro, and salt. Mix well.

Divide the potato mixture into eight equal portions. Dampen your hands a little and roll each portion in turn between your palms to make a ball. Make a dent in the ball, fill it with a tiny amount of the mint and onion filling, cover the filling and flatten each ball gently to form a burger shape.

Just before frying these patties, whisk the egg and season it lightly. Heat a large, nonstick skillet and grease it with half the oil. When the pan is fairly hot, dip a potato patty into the egg and put it in the pan. Add three more patties in the same way.

Let them sizzle for a minute or so, then turn them over and cook the other side until they are crisp and golden brown. Cook the remaining patties in the same way.

COOK'S TIP
The patties freeze well, ready for thawing and reheating when needed. They go well with home-made tomato sauce or any of the chili sauces on page 174.

VEGETABLE SAMOSAS

Serves 4

INGREDIENTS

¾ cup finely diced potatoes

1 tbsp corn or sunflower oil

1 onion, finely chopped

1 garlic clove, crushed

2 red Anaheim chiles, seeded and finely chopped

1 bird's eye (Thai) chile, seeded and very finely chopped

1 tsp ground cumin

1 tsp ground coriander

1 cup shelled peas, thawed if frozen

1 red bell pepper, seeded and diced

1 tbsp apricot or fruit chutney

1 tbsp freshly chopped cilantro

4 sheets filo pastry dough

vegetable oil for deep-frying

chile flowers and fresh cilantro, for the garnish

Cook the diced potatoes in boiling salted water for 5 to 8 minutes, or until just tender. Drain and set aside.

Heat the oil in a skillet and gently sauté the onion, garlic, and chiles for 3 minutes. Add the spices and sauté for 3 minutes more.

Remove from the heat and stir in the potatoes, peas, red bell pepper, chutney, and cilantro. Mix well.

Cut the filo pastry sheets in half lengthwise to make 8 strips, each 10 × 4 inches. Place 1½ tbsp of the filling at one end of each strip and fold over diagonally to form a triangle. Continue folding along the strip, sealing the edges with water.

Heat the oil to 325°F and fry the samosas in batches for about 5 minutes, or until golden. Drain on paper towels. Serve hot or cold, garnished with chile flowers and sprigs of cilantro.

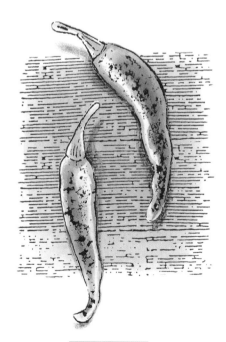

SKILLET CORNBREAD WITH BACON AND JALAPEÑOS

Serves 8

This traditional cornbread is flavored with jalapeño chiles. It is baked in a sizzling-hot skillet,
and seasoned with bits of fried bacon.

INGREDIENTS

4 bacon strips

2½ cups cornmeal

¾ cup all-purpose flour

1½ tsp salt

1 tbsp baking powder

2 tbsp sugar

2 cups milk

½ cup melted butter, or butter and bacon fat

2 eggs, lightly beaten

4 jalapeño chiles, seeded and ground

Preheat the oven to 425°F. Fry the bacon until crisp in a heavy, 9-inch or 10-inch cast-iron skillet. Lift out the bacon and drain it on paper towels. When the bacon is cool enough to handle, crumble it. Leave about 1 tbsp bacon fat in the skillet. Discard the rest, or combine it with melted butter to make ½ cup fat for the bread mix. Combine the dry ingredients in a mixing bowl.

Brush the bacon fat around the bottom and up the side of the skillet so it is completely oiled. Put the skillet in the oven to heat.

Combine the milk and melted butter (or butter and bacon fat), then add to the eggs. Stir in the chiles. Pour the liquid into the dry ingredients and stir by hand until the batter is well mixed. Stir in the crumbled bacon.

The skillet should be very hot and the bacon fat just short of smoking. Carefully pour the batter into the skillet. It will sizzle as it hits the fat. Return the skillet to the oven and bake the cornbread for 35 to 40 minutes, until it is golden brown. Let cool slightly, then cut into wedges. Serve warm.

FRIED FISH STRIPS WITH CHILE DIPPING SAUCE

Serves 3 to 4

Strips of fish, coated in egg and flour, then shallow fried, make a tasty snack, especially when served with a chili sauce for dipping.

INGREDIENTS

1¼ lb white fish fillets such as cod or flounder

1 plump garlic clove, halved lengthwise

all-purpose flour, seasoned with salt and pepper, for coating

1 to 2 eggs, beaten

oil for frying

DIPPING SAUCE

4 tbsp soy sauce

2 tsp sesame oil

1 tbsp rice vinegar

½ red or green chile, seeded and minced

2 tsp toasted sesame seeds

pinch of sugar

½ to 1 small garlic clove, finely chopped

Rub the fish fillets with the cut side of the garlic halves, then thinly slice the fish diagonally. Have the seasoned flour and beaten egg ready in separate shallow bowls. Make the dipping sauce by mixing all the ingredients in a small bowl.

Coat the fish in seasoned flour, then dip in beaten egg, letting the excess egg drain off.

Heat a shallow layer of oil in a skillet. Add the fish strips, in batches if necessary so they are not crowded, and fry for about 5 minutes, depending on thickness. Drain on paper towels, then serve hot with the dipping sauce.

DEEP-FRIED SHRIMP WITH SPICY TOMATO SALSA

Serves 4

Crisp on the outside, beautifully tender within, jumbo shrimp in batter are irresistible.

INGREDIENTS

¾ cup all-purpose flour

2 tsp black sesame seeds

salt and pepper

I egg, beaten

I to 2 tsp sesame oil

½ to ¾ cup water

12 to 16 raw jumbo shrimp,
in their shells

vegetable oil for deep-frying

SPICY TOMATO SALSA

3 garlic cloves, chopped

2 serrano chiles, chopped

½ onion, chopped

I lb flavorful tomatoes, chopped

2 tbsp freshly chopped parsley

2 tbsp freshly chopped cilantro

salt and ground cumin, to taste

juice of I lime

Make the salsa by mixing all the ingredients in a bowl. Cover and set aside for at least 30 minutes to develop the flavors.

Mix the flour and sesame seeds. Stir in the egg and sesame oil, then add enough of the water to make a light coating batter. Set aside.

Remove the heads and fine legs from the shrimp, leaving the tails intact. With a fine knife-point, slit along the back of each shrimp and remove the dark thread.

Heat the oil in a deep-fat fryer to 350°F. Stir the batter, then dip the shrimp into it, allowing the excess batter to drain off. Deep-fry the shrimp in batches for about 3 to 4 minutes until crisp and brown. Drain on paper towels. Keep hot while frying the remaining shrimp. Serve hot with the salsa.

SOUPS

COCONUT AND GINGER SOUP

Serves 4 to 6

This creamy soup originated in Thailand. Use galangal instead of ginger, if you can find it, as it has a milder flavor and is more fragrant.

INGREDIENTS

5 cups thin coconut milk

1 shallot, finely sliced

1-inch piece gingerroot, peeled and thinly sliced

2 lemongrass stalks, cut into ¾-inch pieces

6 small whole red fresh chiles

3 kaffir lime leaves, torn into small pieces

1 tsp salt

11 oz skinless boneless chicken breasts, cut across into ¼-inch slices

2 cups wiped and sliced mushrooms, oyster if available

2 tbsp lime or lemon juice

½ tsp Thai fish sauce

3 tbsp freshly chopped cilantro leaves, with stems cut into ¾-inch pieces

hot cooked rice, for serving

Pour the coconut milk into a saucepan and bring to a boil. Add the shallot, ginger, lemongrass, chiles, lime leaves, and salt.

When the liquid returns to a boil, add the chicken and bring to a boil again, then add the mushrooms. Bring back to a boil and cook for 2 minutes or until the chicken is fully cooked. Remove from the heat and stir in the lime or lemon juice, fish sauce, and cilantro leaves and stems.

Serve over hot cooked rice in bowls. Garnish with extra small red chiles, if you like.

COLD AVOCADO SOUP

Serves 4 to 6

Cold and creamy, with very good color, this is an excellent choice for summer.

INGREDIENTS

1 or 2 green Anaheim chiles

1 tbsp oil

3 large ripe avocados

⅔ cup chicken or vegetable stock

1¼ cups light cream

⅔ cup milk

1 to 2 tbsp lime juice

salt and white pepper

freshly snipped chives and sour cream,
for the garnish

Preheat the broiler to high. Cut the chiles in half and discard the seeds. Place in a broiler pan, skin-side uppermost, and drizzle with the oil. Broil for 5 minutes, or until the skin has blistered. Remove from the heat and leave to cool.

Discard the skin and membrane from the chiles and roughly chop. Put into a food processor. Peel and seed the avocados, then roughly chop and add to the processor with the stock. Process to a smooth purée.

With the machine still running at low speed, add the cream through the feeder tube, then the milk.

Stir in the lime juice and seasoning to taste. Pour into a soup tureen and chill for at least 1 hour. Serve garnished with snipped chives and sour cream.

HOT-AND-SOUR SHRIMP SOUP

Serves 4 to 6

This is a very fragrant soup from Thailand. Some recipes use tamarind to give the sour taste; others, like this one, use lime juice.

INGREDIENTS

3¾ cups fish or chicken stock

2 lemongrass stalks

1-inch piece gingerroot, peeled and grated

2 or 3 bird's eye (Thai) chiles, seeded and chopped

few fresh kaffir lime leaves

1 large carrot, cut into julienne strips

1 lb raw jumbo shrimp, shelled and deveined

1½ cups wiped and sliced shiitake mushrooms

2 tbsp lime juice

1 tbsp Thai fish sauce

1 tsp chili paste

1 cup bean sprouts

2 tbsp freshly chopped cilantro

Put the stock into a large pan. Remove the outer leaves from the lemongrass and finely chop. Add to the stock with the ginger, chiles, and lime leaves. Bring to a boil, then reduce the heat and simmer for 10 minutes.

Add the carrot, shrimp, and mushrooms to the pan. Simmer for 5 to 8 minutes more, or until the shrimp have turned pink.

Mix the lime juice, fish sauce, and chili paste together, then stir into the pan and continue simmering for 1 to 2 minutes. Add the bean sprouts and chopped cilantro, stir once and then serve.

FISH SOUP WITH CHILES

Serves 4

Use one type of fish for this soup, or a selection. Cod, haddock, red snapper, and sea bass are all suitable.

INGREDIENTS

1 tbsp oil

1 large onion, finely chopped

1 garlic clove, crushed

2 celery stalks, trimmed and chopped

2 de agua chiles, seeded and chopped

1½ cups peeled, seeded, and chopped tomatoes

1 tbsp tomato paste

2 cups fish stock

1 lb white fish fillets, skinned and cut into bite-size pieces

salt and pepper

flat-leaf parsley, for the garnish

Heat the oil in a large pan and sauté the onion, garlic, and chiles for 5 minutes, or until softened. Add the chopped tomatoes. Stir in the tomato paste and sauté for 3 minutes more.

Pour in the stock and bring to a boil. Reduce the heat and simmer gently for 10 minutes.

Add the fish and simmer for 5 minutes more, or until the fish is cooked. Season to taste, and serve in heated bowls, garnished with flat-leaf parsley.

▶ *Hot-and-Sour Shrimp Soup*

TORTILLA SOUP

Serves 4

This is a typical example of a Mexican "dry" soup. The name does not mean that there is very little liquid, but rather that the soup contains some sort of dry ingredient, like pasta, rice or even slightly stale tortillas, to absorb some of the stock.

INGREDIENTS

2 tomatoes, halved

2 tbsp olive oil

1 medium onion, chopped

2 garlic cloves

4 cups chicken stock

lard or oil for deep-frying

12 corn tortillas, preferably a little stale

2 or 3 dried pasilla chiles

salt and pepper

avocado slices and sour cream, for the garnish

Preheat the broiler. Arrange the tomatoes, cut sides up, in a broiler pan. Broil until beginning to brown. Set aside.

Heat half the olive oil in a pan. Add the onion and garlic and sauté for 5 to 7 minutes until softened and golden brown. Tip the contents of the pan into a blender or food processor, add the broiled tomatoes and process to a purée.

Heat the remaining olive oil in the pan and cook the puréed tomato mixture until thick, stirring constantly.

Stir in the stock and bring to a boil, then reduce the heat and simmer for 30 minutes.

While the soup is simmering, heat the lard or oil for deep frying. Cut the tortillas into 2- x ½-inch strips. Remove the seeds and veins from the chiles and tear them into pieces. Deep-fry the tortilla strips, with the chiles, until the strips are crisp and brown and the chiles are crumbly. Lift out and drain on paper towels.

Season the soup. Spoon the crisp tortillas and chiles into heated bowls and ladle the soup on top. Serve at once, garnished with avocado slices and sour cream. Offer lime wedges for squeezing into the soup, if you like.

CHICKEN AND CHILE SOUP

Serves 4 to 6

This lightly curried soup is quite filling, so serve it solo, with crusty bread, or balance the rest of the meal by following it
with a fish dish or main course salad.

INGREDIENTS

1 tsp oil

1 tsp green curry paste

2½ cups chicken stock

⅔ cup coconut milk

1 or 2 bird's eye (Thai) chiles, seeded and chopped

2 lemongrass stalks, outer leaves removed and finely chopped

4 kaffir lime leaves

1-inch piece gingerroot, peeled and finely grated

12 oz skinless, boneless chicken breasts, cut into thin strips

1 cup cut green beans

3-inch piece cucumber, peeled if preferred and cut into strips

½ cup cooked fragrant rice

1 to 2 tsp honey

4 tbsp light cream (optional)

Heat the oil in a large pan and fry the curry paste gently for 3 minutes, stirring occasionally.

Add the stock with the coconut milk, chiles, lemongrass, lime leaves, and ginger. Bring to a boil and boil for 3 minutes. Reduce the heat, add the chicken strips and simmer for 5 to 10 minutes, or until the chicken is cooked.

Add the green beans and cucumber with the rice and honey. Simmer for 5 minutes more, or until the vegetables are tender.

Stir in the cream, if using, and serve at once in heated bowls.

CHICKEN AND AVOCADO SOUP

Serves 4

This simple soup comes from Mexico, where it is served in a variety of ways. Chicken and avocado are essential, chiles are optional (but almost always included) and the amount of garlic varies from a single clove to a whole head.

INGREDIENTS

4 cups chicken stock

8 oz skinless, boneless chicken breast, cut into thin strips

1 or 2 dried red de Arbol chiles

1 to 5 garlic cloves

3 tbsp water

½ to 1 tsp salt

1 avocado

freshly chopped cilantro, for the garnish

Pour the stock into a pan and bring it to a boil; reduce the heat, add the chicken and simmer for 3 to 5 minutes until it is cooked.

Remove the seeds and veins from the chiles. Tear them into pieces and place in a mortar with the garlic and water. Grind to a paste, then press through a strainer into the stock. Stir, simmer for a couple of minutes, and add salt to taste.

Peel the avocado and slice into strips. Separate the slices carefully before dropping them into the soup, or they will stick together. They will sink for a few moments, then float to the surface. When they do, the soup is ready. Serve it in a heated tureen, garnished with cilantro.

COOK'S TIP
You can make the soup using cooked chicken. Simply reheat it in the simmering stock before adding the chili and garlic paste.

SPICY CHICKEN SOUP

Serves 4

Adding fresh vegetables to this clear chicken soup toward the end of cooking creates a colorful and nutritious dish. The pepper sauce adds a touch of fire, but don't overdo it or you'll really be going for the burn.

INGREDIENTS

3 lb chicken

5 garlic cloves, peeled

1 onion, diced

2 celery stalks, including leaves, diced

2 carrots, diced

1 parsnip, diced

6 cups water

½ tsp freshly snipped fresh basil

½ tsp curry powder

dash of Hot, Hot, Hot Pepper Sauce (page 177)

1 tsp freshly chopped cilantro

salt and pepper

1 red jalapeño chile, seeded and thinly sliced, for the garnish (optional)

Place the chicken in a large pan. Add the whole peeled garlic cloves and half the vegetables. Pour in the water to cover the chicken, then add the basil, curry powder, hot pepper sauce, and cilantro, with salt and pepper to taste. Bring to a boil, then immediately reduce the heat and simmer uncovered for about 2 hours.

Skim the fat off the top of the soup and strain it into a clean pan. Refrigerate the cooked chicken for later use.

Add the remaining vegetables to the soup. Simmer for 10 minutes more, or until the vegetables are tender. Serve in heated bowls. Garnish with the fresh chile, if using.

COOK'S TIP

For a more robust soup, add some of the cooked chicken and some noodles or rice.

CALLALOO

Serves 4 to 6

This Caribbean soup takes its name from what is traditionally its chief ingredient, the leaves of the tuberous taro or callaloo plant. Cooks outside the Caribbean have found that fresh spinach, Swiss chard, and kale are quite similar to callaloo and a lot easier to track down. Mint-green in color and with a subtle, sharp flavor, the soup makes a refreshing opener for any meal.

INGREDIENTS

8 oz fresh spinach, Swiss chard or kale

4 oz okra, sliced (optional)

1 large eggplant, peeled and chopped into bite-size pieces

4 cups water

1 tbsp vegetable oil

2 onions, finely chopped

2 garlic cloves, minced

½ tsp thyme

¼ tsp allspice

2 tbsp snipped chives

1 fresh hot chile, seeded and chopped, or 1 tbsp hot pepper sauce

1 tbsp white wine vinegar

1 cup coconut milk

salt and pepper

Wash and drain the greens, discarding the stems. Chop the leaves into pieces. Place in a large, heavy pan with the okra, if using, and the eggplant.

Add the water and bring to a boil. Reduce the heat and simmer for about 15 minutes until the vegetables are tender. (If you have added okra, check frequently as this vegetables tends to become glutinous if overcooked.)

Heat the oil in a heavy skillet and sauté the onions and garlic until the onions are translucent. Add to the pan with the remaining ingredients, and simmer for about 5 minutes more. Purée in a blender or food processor, reheat if necessary and serve.

RED PEPPER AND CHILE SOUP

Serves 4

With its glorious color, this soup makes a great opener for a special meal.

INGREDIENTS

2 red bell peppers

2 red jalapeño chiles

2 tbsp sunflower oil

I onion, finely chopped

I garlic clove, minced

2½ cups vegetable or chicken stock

8 oz ripe tomatoes, peeled, seeded, and chopped

salt and pepper

2 tbsp light cream

chopped red bell pepper, for the garnish

Preheat the broiler. Cut the peppers and chiles in half, discarding the seeds. Place, skin-side up, on a sheet of foil in a broiler pan. Drizzle with I tbsp of the oil and broil for 5 to 10 minutes, or until the skins have blistered. Remove from the heat and place in a bowl. Cover with several paper towels and leave to cool. When cool, remove the skins from the peppers and chiles and roughly chop the flesh.

Heat the remaining oil in a pan and sauté the onion and garlic for 5 minutes, or until transparent but not browned. Add the chopped peppers and chiles and pour over the stock. Add the tomatoes to the pan, with seasoning to taste. Bring to a boil, then lower the heat, cover and simmer gently for 15 minutes, or until the peppers are really soft.

Leave to cool, then purée in a food processor. If the soup is to be served hot, return it to the rinsed pan, check the seasoning and reheat gently. If it is to be served cold, chill for at least 1 hour.

To serve, add the cream and swirl lightly, then sprinkle with a little chopped red bell pepper.

APPETIZERS

KOREAN CRAB CAKES WITH GINGER DIPPING SAUCE

Serves 4

INGREDIENTS

2 potatoes

1½ garlic cloves, minced

1 fresh red chile, seeded and finely chopped

1-inch piece fresh gingerroot, grated

3 scallions, finely chopped

1½ cups white and brown crab meat, thawed and drained if frozen

finely grated peel of ½ lime

2 tbsp freshly chopped cilantro

salt and pepper

1½ tbsp sesame seeds

1 cup fresh bread crumbs, for coating

flour for coating

1 egg, beaten

oil for deep-frying

GINGER DIPPING SAUCE

thinly pared cucumber curl and fresh herbs, for the garnish

6 tbsp rice vinegar

1-inch piece fresh gingerroot, grated

2 scallions, white part only, finely chopped

2 tbsp dark soy sauce

2 tsp sugar

Make the sauce by mixing all the ingredients in a small bowl. Set aside.

Cook the potatoes in their skins in boiling water until tender. Drain. When cool enough to handle, peel the potatoes and mash them.

Put the mashed potato in a bowl. Add the garlic, chile, ginger, scallions, crab meat, lime peel, and cilantro. Season well with salt and pepper. Form into eight round cakes about the size of golf balls. Chill for 30 minutes.

Stir the sesame seeds into the bread crumbs. Spread out on a shallow dish or a sheet of foil. Have the flour and egg ready in shallow bowls. Coat the crab cakes in the flour, then the egg and finally in the bread crumb mixture, pressing the crumbs on firmly.

Heat the oil for deep-frying to about 325°F. Fry the crab cakes in batches for about 8 minutes until golden. Transfer to paper towels to drain and keep hot while frying the remaining crab cakes. Serve immediately, garnished with the cucumber curl and fresh herbs. Offer the dipping sauce separately.

COOK'S TIP

Cut a long cucumber in half, then use a vegetable parer to pare off a long, wide ribbon including both flesh and peel. Loop the strip on the plate. Alternatively, garnish the crab cakes with a zucchini concertina: head and stem a straight zucchini then push a wooden skewer through the center, right along its length. Rotating the skewer, slice the zucchini thinly, then pull the skewer out.

SHRIMP RELLENOS

Serves 4

"Rellenos" is a Spanish word meaning stuffed. If canned chiles are unavailable, use large fresh ones that have been seeded and blanched.

INGREDIENTS

8 to 12 drained, tinned, large, green chiles

8 oz shelled shrimp, finely chopped

4 scallions, trimmed and chopped

3 green jalapeño chiles, seeded and finely chopped

½ cup grated hard cheese, such as Cheddar

1 small red apple, cored and finely chopped

grated peel of 1 lemon

salt and pepper

3 to 4 tbsp prepared mayonnaise

salad leaves and sliced red jalapeño chiles, for the garnish

P at the canned chiles dry with paper towels and make a slit down one side. Discard the seeds if necessary, then rinse and pat dry again.

Mix the shrimp, scallions, chiles, cheese, apple, and lemon peel in a bowl. Add salt and pepper to taste. Stir in the mayonnaise and mix well.

Use the shrimp mixture to stuff the chiles. Arrange on a serving platter and garnish with salad leaves and thinly sliced red jalapeños.

SCALLOPS WITH HABANERO AND MANGO SLICES

Serves 4

The delicate flavor of the scallops is enhanced, not overwhelmed, by the salsa.

INGREDIENTS

12 large fresh scallops, cleaned

4 tbsp unsalted butter

1 tbsp olive or sunflower oil

assorted bitter salad leaves, such as arugula, escarole, radicchio, and endive

edible flowers, such as nasturtiums, for the garnish

SALSA

1 small ripe mango, peeled, seed removed and finely chopped

3 scallions, trimmed and finely chopped

2 orange habanero chiles, seeded and chopped

2-inch piece cucumber, seeded and finely diced

2 tomatoes peeled, seeded and finely chopped

1 to 2 tsp dark brown or molasses sugar

2 tbsp freshly chopped chervil

M ix all the ingredients for the salsa in a bowl and cover. Chill for 15 minutes. Cut the scallops into thick slices. Rinse, drain and pat dry with paper towels. Heat the butter and oil in a skillet. When the butter starts to bubble add the scallops and cook gently for 2 to 3 minutes, or until just cooked. Drain. Arrange the salad leaves on a serving platter or in a bowl and top with the scallops. Garnish with the edible flowers and serve with the salsa.

▶ *Shrimp Rellenos*

CRISPY ANCHOVIES

Serves 4

The dried anchovies for this dish are about the size of European whitebait and are deep-fried in the same way. They can be found in most Japanese supermarkets. If the anchovies are very salty, rub or rinse off excess salt before frying. Serve deep-fried anchovies with a sweet/hot sauce to contrast with their saltiness.

INGREDIENTS

1 garlic clove, finely chopped

1 small onion, chopped

1 fresh red chile, seeded

¾ tsp salt

1½ tsp sugar

2 tbsp vegetable oil, plus extra for deep-frying

about 4 oz dried anchovies, heads removed if liked, rinsed if necessary

fresh cilantro leaves, for the garnish

Combine the garlic, onion, chile, and salt in a mortar and grind to a paste with a pestle. Stir in the sugar; set aside.

Heat the 2 tbsp vegetable oil in a large skillet. Add the onion paste and cook for 3 to 4 minutes.

Meanwhile, heat the oil for deep-frying to 350°F. Add the anchovies, in batches if necessary, and fry for 20–30 seconds until very crisp and lightly colored.

Drain the anchovies on paper towels, then tip into the skillet and heat through, shaking the pan so that they become coated in the spicy garlic paste. Transfer to a serving bowl, garnish with the cilantro leaves and serve at once.

COOK'S TIP

Tossing the fried anchovies with the sauce gives them a wonderful flavor. Offer lime wedges for squeezing, if you like.

MEXICAN MINI-MEATBALLS

Serves 12

These spicy meatballs — albondiguitas — make an excellent appetizer and look very colorful when presented on a platter with a selection of dipping sauces and raw vegetables.

INGREDIENTS

1 lb lean ground beef

12 oz ground pork

½ cup cooked rice

1 small onion, minced

2 garlic cloves, minced

1 red jalapeño chile, seeded and minced

1 tsp chili powder, or to taste

2 tsp freshly chopped cilantro

salt and pepper

2 eggs, beaten

oil for deep-frying

whole green chiles and olives, for the garnish

crudités and dipping sauces, for serving

Mix the ground beef and pork in a bowl. Add the rice, onion, garlic, and chile, with the chili powder and cilantro. Season with salt and pepper.

Add enough of the beaten egg to bind the mixture, then mix well, using a wooden spoon. Make sure that the onion and chile are well distributed.

Form the mixture into small rounds, about the size of golf balls, rolling them between the palms of your hands. Make sure your hands are clean.

Heat the oil for deep-frying to 350°F. Add the meatballs, in batches if necessary, and fry for 4–5 minutes until cooked through. Check by lifting out one of the meatballs and cutting it in half. As soon as a batch of meatballs is cooked, drain on paper towels and keep hot while cooking successive batches.

Pile the meatballs onto a platter and garnish with whole green chiles, ripe and stuffed olives, and a selection of crudités. Offer at least two dipping sauces; one mild and one hot, with sour cream or plain yogurt.

COOK'S TIP
Make larger meatballs, fry them in oil until browned, then poach them in a rich spicy tomato sauce for a delicious family meal. For more sophisticated occasions, hide a deseeded olive in the center of each meatball.

SAUTÉED MUSHROOMS WITH CHILI SALSA

Serves 4

As easy to eat as they are to prepare, these toast treats make fine appetizers.

INGREDIENTS

6 tbsp virgin olive oil

1 garlic clove, minced

2 de agua chiles, seeded and sliced

2 shallots, thinly sliced

2½ cups wiped and sliced assorted
wild mushrooms

1 cup wiped button mushrooms

1½ cups peeled, seeded and chopped
plum tomatoes

1 tbsp freshly chopped basil

salt and pepper

1 ciabatta loaf, sliced

Red Chili Sauce (page 175)

sprigs of fresh basil, for the garnish

Heat 4 tbsp of the oil in a skillet and gently sauté the garlic, chiles, and shallots for 5 minutes, or until the shallots are soft and transparent. Add the mushrooms and continue to cook for 4 to 5 minutes. Stir in the tomatoes, basil and seasoning to taste. Heat through for 1 to 2 minutes.

Meanwhile, drizzle the ciabatta slices with the remaining oil and broil lightly. Arrange the mushroom mixture on the toasted bread and serve with the chili sauce. Garnish with sprigs of basil.

CRAB-STUFFED TOMATOES

Serves 4

For an authentic Caribbean flavor, use the fiery pepper sauce recommended, but if you feel this makes the appetizer too hot to handle, use a bottled hot pepper sauce instead.

INGREDIENTS

2 cups crab meat, thawed and drained
if frozen

⅔ cup seeded and chopped ripe
tomatoes

⅔ cup diced seedless cucumber

2 hard-cooked eggs, chopped

⅔ cup mayonnaise

Hot, Hot, Hot Pepper Sauce
(page 177) to taste

2 tbsp sour cream

2 tsp lime juice

1 tbsp snipped chives

salt and pepper

4 tomatoes

1 soft-leafed lettuce,
rinsed and drained

In a bowl, mix together the crab, chopped tomatoes, cucumber, and eggs. Cover and chill. In a separate bowl, mix the mayonnaise with the pepper sauce, sour cream, lime juice, and chives. Stir in salt and pepper to taste, then cover and chill.

Without cutting all the way through the bottoms, core the whole tomatoes and cut them into sixths, separating the wedges slightly to form tulip shapes. Line four plates with the lettuce, center a tomato on each and divide the crab mixture among them. Spoon a little of the flavored mayonnaise over each filled tomato and hand around the remaining mayonnaise separately.

► *Sautéed mushrooms*

THAI LETTUCE PACKAGES

Serves 4

Good things come in small packages: that is certainly true of these delicious treats.

INGREDIENTS

1 tbsp corn or sunflower oil

1 garlic clove, crushed

2 lemongrass stalks, outer leaves removed and finely chopped

1-inch piece gingerroot, peeled and grated

2 to 3 bird's eye (Thai) red chiles, seeded and chopped

8 oz shredded skinless, boneless chicken breast (about 1½ cups)

1 tbsp soy sauce

2 tsp Thai fish sauce

1 cup bean sprouts

1 small iceberg lettuce, separated into leaves

DIPPING SAUCE

2 tbsp Thai fish sauce

2 garlic cloves, crushed

1 to 2 tbsp sugar

2 tbsp lime juice

2 tbsp white wine vinegar

1 bird's eye (Thai) chile, seeded and finely chopped

Mix all the ingredients for the sauce together in a bowl. Cover and leave for at least 30 minutes for the flavors to develop.

Heat the oil in a wok or large saucepan and stir-fry the garlic, lemongrass, ginger, and chiles for 2 minutes.

Add the chicken and continue to stir-fry for 5 minutes, or until the chicken is cooked. Add the soy sauce and fish sauce, stir once, then add the bean sprouts and stir-fry for 30 seconds more.

Arrange a heaped spoonful of the chicken mixture on each lettuce leaf and drizzle with a little of the sauce. Roll up to form a package. Serve the filled packages on a platter, with the remaining dipping sauce.

DEEP-FRIED BRIE WITH SPICY APRICOT SALSA

Serves 4

Deep-fried cheeses are very popular, especially when served with a spicy salsa.

INGREDIENTS

8 oz Brie cheese

1 large egg, beaten

2 cups fresh white bread crumbs

oil for deep-frying

fresh salad leaves, for the garnish

SALSA

1 tbsp sunflower oil

1 small onion, finely chopped

1 red bell pepper, seeded and finely chopped

1 red fresno chile, seeded and finely chopped

¾ cup finely chopped no-need-to-soak dried apricots

⅔ cup orange juice

Cut the Brie into four equal portions. Have the beaten egg ready in one shallow bowl and the bread crumbs in another. Dip the Brie in the beaten egg, then coat in the bread crumbs. Cover lightly and place in the refrigerator while you make the salsa.

Heat the sunflower oil in a pan and gently sauté the onion, red bell pepper and chile for 5 minutes. Stir in the apricots and orange juice. Simmer for 15 minutes, or until a chunky consistency is reached.

Heat the oil for deep-frying to 340°F and fry the coated Brie portions for 3 to 4 minutes, or until golden. Drain on paper towels. Garnish with salad leaves and serve with the apricot salsa.

HOT STUFFED CHILES

Serves 4

Chiles play a leading role in this delicious appetizer. Serve with crispy "seaweed," made by deep-frying shreds of collar greens, then tossing the shreds with a mixture of superfine sugar and salt.

INGREDIENTS

1 lb lean ground pork (about 2 cups)

1 garlic clove, minced

½-inch piece fresh gingerroot, peeled and finely chopped

4 scallions, finely chopped

2 tsp toasted sesame seeds

2 to 3 tsp soy sauce

16 to 20 large fresh red chiles

seasoned flour, for coating

1 large egg, beaten

oil for shallow frying

Mix the pork, garlic, ginger, scallions, sesame seeds and soy sauce very well.

Cut the chiles in half lengthwise, through the stem and carefully remove the seeds leaving the chile "boats" intact. Break off small pieces of the meat mixture, form into torpedo shapes and use to stuff the chiles, packing the meat mixture in firmly.

Have ready one shallow bowl containing seasoned flour and another containing the beaten egg. Roll the stuffed chiles in the flour to give an even coating, then dip in the egg.

Heat a ½-inch layer of oil in a skillet. Add the chiles in batches and fry for 4 to 5 minutes on each side until golden brown and cooked through. Remove from the oil with a slotted spoon and drain on paper towels. Serve hot.

COOK'S TIP
Take care when turning the stuffed chiles over that the filling does not fall out.

FISH & SEAFOOD

ORANGE- AND CHILE-MARINATED SARDINES

Serves 4

Sardines cooked this way are simply delicious. Use lime juice instead of orange, if you prefer.

INGREDIENTS

8 to 12 fresh sardines, cleaned

½ cup orange juice

4 tbsp olive oil

4 green jalapeño chiles, seeded and finely sliced

1 tbsp soft light brown sugar

few sprigs of fresh rosemary

orange wedges and sprigs of fresh rosemary, for the garnish

Wipe or lightly rinse the sardines and pat dry with paper towels. Place in a shallow dish. Mix the orange juice, oil, chiles, and sugar and pour over the sardines. Tear the sprigs of rosemary into small pieces and scatter over the top. Cover and chill for at least 2 hours, turning the sardines occasionally.

Preheat the broiler to medium and line the broiler rack with foil. Drain the sardines and place on the foil-lined rack. Broil for 3 to 4 minutes, or until cooked through, basting with the marinade at least once during broiling. Garnish with orange wedges and sprigs of rosemary.

COOK'S TIP
The sardines can be cooked on a barbecue for 3 to 4 minutes once the coals are ready. It is best to place them in a hinged fish grill.

CALYPSO COD STEAKS

Serves 6

These cod steaks have plenty of zip, thanks to the chile. You can cook salmon in the same way. If you do not have a fresh chile, use hot pepper sauce instead.

INGREDIENTS

3 tbsp lime juice

2 tbsp olive oil

2 tsp minced garlic

1 small red chile, seeded and minced

6 cod or salmon steaks, about 6 oz each

In a bowl, whisk together the lime juice, olive oil, garlic, and chile.

Brush the broiler rack with oil and preheat the broiler. Broil the steaks for about 10 to 12 minutes on one side, basting frequently with the sauce, then turn and cook on the other side for 10 to 12 minutes more, again basting frequently, until done. Pour some of the cooking juices over the steaks when serving.

▶ *Marinated Sardines*

FISH WITH BLACK BEANS

Serves 4

Salted black beans are available in cans from Chinese food stores. They make an excellent marinade and sauce for fish.

INGREDIENTS

2 lb flounder, whiting or finnan haddie fillet, skinned

3 tbsp salted black beans

⅓ cup dry sherry

3 tbsp light soy sauce

1 tsp sesame oil

¼ cup cornstarch

3 tbsp oil

2-inch piece fresh gingerroot, peeled and cut in fine strips

1 fresh green chile, seeded and cut into rings

1 garlic clove, minced

1 piece lemongrass or strip of pared lemon peel

1 bunch green onions, cut diagonally into strips

⅓ cup water

Cut the fish across into ½-inch wide strips and place these in a large shallow dish. Sprinkle the salted black beans, sherry, soy sauce, and sesame oil over the fish. Cover the dish and leave the strips to marinate for 2 to 3 hours.

When you are ready to cook the fish, drain the strips well, reserving the marinade. Gently toss the strips in the cornstarch.

Heat the oil in a wok or skillet, then stir-fry the ginger, chile, garlic, and lemongrass or peel over medium heat for 4 to 5 minutes, to extract their flavor. Add the fish strips to the pan and stir-fry them carefully, avoiding breaking the strips, until they are lightly browned.

Add all the green onions and continue to stir-fry for 2 minutes, until the onions are cooked. Add the water to the reserved marinade and pour the mixture into the wok or skillet. Bring to a boil over high heat, reduce the heat and stir-fry for 1 minute, then serve.

SQUID WITH HOT PEPPER SAUCE

Serves 4

INGREDIENTS

4 dried ancho chiles

1½ lb cleaned squid

2 shallots, chopped

2 garlic cloves, crushed

2 red habanero chiles, seeded and chopped

2 tbsp corn or sunflower oil

2¼ cups peeled, seeded and chopped plum tomatoes

juice of 2 limes

2 to 3 tsp soft light brown sugar

a few sprigs of fresh oregano

Roast the dried ancho chiles in a nonstick skillet for 2 to 3 minutes, taking care not to let them scorch. Tip into a bowl and add hot (not boiling) water. Soak for at least 10 minutes, until soft.

Prepare the squid by cutting off the tentacles and rinsing. Remove and discard the head, internal organs, and central transparent quill. Rub off the purplish outer skin. Rinse the body, then slice it. Slice the tentacles too.

Put the shallots, garlic, habañeros and drained ancho chiles into a mortar and grind to a paste with a pestle.

Heat the oil in a wok or large pan and gently cook the paste for 3 minutes. Add the tomatoes, lime juice, and sugar, and cook for 10 to 12 minutes, or until a thick sauce forms.

Add the oregano, reserving a little for the garnish. Stir in the squid and simmer for 5 minutes, or until the squid is tender. Take care not to overcook, or the squid will become rubbery. Serve sprinkled with the remaining oregano.

YOGURT-SPICED FISH

Serves 4

INGREDIENTS

4 haddock or cod steaks,
about 6 oz each, cubed

1 tbsp corn or sunflower oil

2 garlic cloves, crushed

3 red jalapeño chiles, seeded and finely
sliced

1 tsp turmeric

1 tsp ground cumin

1 tsp ground coriander

1 tsp ground fenugreek

6 cardamom pods, crushed

⅔ cup plain yogurt

2 tbsp flaked almonds, toasted

fresh herbs, for the garnish

Place the fish cubes in a shallow dish. Heat the oil in a skillet and gently sauté the garlic and chiles for 3 minutes, stirring frequently. Add the spices and cook gently for 3 to 4 minutes more. Off the heat, stir in the yogurt. Pour the mixture over the fish, then cover and leave to marinate in the refrigerator for at least 1 hour, turning the fish after 30 minutes.

Preheat the broiler to medium and line the broiler rack with foil. Drain the fish from the yogurt mixture and thread onto skewers. Broil for 3 to 4 minutes, or until tender and the fish flakes easily. Serve sprinkled with the almonds and garnished with fresh herbs.

SALMON STEAKS WITH THAI-STYLE SAUCE

Serves 4

INGREDIENTS

4 salmon steaks, about 6 oz each

1 small onion, sliced

2 bay leaves

few sprigs of parsley

4 or 5 black peppercorns

⅔ cup dry white wine

1 tbsp white wine vinegar

⅔ cup water

lemon twists, for the garnish

THAI-STYLE SAUCE

2 tbsp olive oil

1 garlic clove, minced

1-inch piece gingerroot, peeled and grated

1 cup shelled raw peanuts

2 red Thai chiles, seeded and sliced

2 tsp soft dark brown sugar

1¼ cups vegetable stock

1 tbsp lemon juice

Wipe the salmon steaks and set them aside. Place the onion, bay leaves, parsley, peppercorns, wine and vinegar in a skillet. Add the water and bring to a boil. Reduce the heat and simmer for 10 minutes. Strain and reserve the liquid until you are ready to cook the fish.

Heat the oil for the sauce in the skillet and sauté the garlic and ginger for 2 minutes. Add the peanuts and fry gently for 10 minutes, or until golden.

Tip the contents of the skillet into a food processor and add the chiles, brown sugar, stock, and lemon juice. Process to a purée, then scrape into a small saucepan and simmer for 8 to 10 minutes, or until slightly reduced.

Pour the strained spiced vinegar into the cleaned skillet and add the fish. Bring to a boil, then cover and reduce the heat to a very gentle simmer. Cook for 3 to 4 minutes, or until the fish is cooked. Drain and arrange on serving plates. Spoon a little of the sauce over each portion. Garnish with lemon twists.

HOT CHILE

STEAMED FISH WITH LEMON AND CHILE

Serves 4

The combination of lime juice and fresh chiles in the topping give this dish a refreshing spicy tartness.

INGREDIENTS

1 whole sea bass (about 2 lb), cleaned

½ cup lime juice

2 tbsp chopped small fresh green chiles

2 tbsp minced garlic

2 tbsp Thai fish sauce

½ tbsp salt

1 tsp sugar

¼ cup cilantro (leaves and cut stems)

lime slices, for the garnish

Steam the fish whole for 20 to 30 minutes until tender but firm. Meanwhile, mix all the remaining ingredients except the cilantro in a bowl. When the fish is cooked, place it on a serving platter and immediately spoon the lime juice mixture all over (the fish must be very hot when the sauce is added). Sprinkle with the cilantro, garnish with the lime slices and serve.

COOK'S TIP

If you do not have a steamer big enough to hold the fish, sprinkle it lightly with a mixture of lime juice and oil, wrap it in foil, support it in a roasting pan and cook for about 45 minutes at 350°F.

FRIED FISH WITH CHILI TOPPING

Serves 4 to 6

The scored flesh of the fish traps the spicy sauce, which is poured on top at the last minute.

INGREDIENTS

8 garlic cloves, chopped

5 fresh yellow chiles, chopped

2 lb whole sea bass, cleaned

½ tsp each salt and ground white pepper

flour for dusting

oil for deep-frying

½ cup fresh basil leaves

¼ cup corn oil

½ cup chicken stock

2 fresh red chiles, quartered lengthwise

1 tbsp tamarind juice or vinegar

2 tsp sugar

1 tsp Thai fish sauce

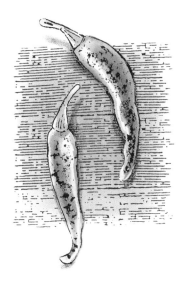

Put the garlic and yellow chiles in a mortar and pound with a pestle to make a paste.

Score the fish on both sides five or six times, sprinkle on the salt and pepper and dust with the flour. Heat the oil for deep-frying to 350°F and fry the fish for 7 to 10 minutes, until crisp but tender inside. Lift out the fish, drain it on paper towels, and put it in a serving dish and keep hot. Add the basil leaves to the hot oil and fry for 1 minute until crisp. Drain and reserve for garnishing.

Heat the corn oil in a skillet and fry the garlic and chili paste for 1 minute. Add the remaining ingredients and boil lightly for minutes until slightly thick. Pour on top of the fish and sprinkle over the fried basil.

Shrimp with Okra

Serves 4

Use baby okra, if you can find them. They will not release as much sap as the larger, sliced pods.

Ingredients

12 oz okra (prepared weight)
2 tbsp oil
2 onions
2 or 3 whole dried chiles
½ tsp cumin seeds
4 garlic cloves, chopped
¼ tsp turmeric
½ tsp chili powder
½ tsp ground ginger
3 tomatoes, chopped
8 oz shelled shrimp
1 or 2 fresh green chiles, slit
1 tsp salt
2 tbsp tamarind pulp or lemon juice
2 tbsp freshly chopped cilantro

Wash the okra and pat dry with paper towels. Head and stem them, then chop into ½-inch slices.

Heat the oil in a saucepan and lightly fry the onions with the dried chiles and cumin seeds. Add the garlic, turmeric, chili powder, and ginger. Stir the mixture well and cook two to three minutes, stirring continuously.

Add the okra and tomatoes, stirring to coat them well with the spices. Cover the pan and simmer the mixture gently for 5 to 7 minutes, stirring occasionally.

Stir in the shrimp with the slit green chiles and the salt. Cook for 5 minutes more, than add the tamarind pulp or lemon juice and cilantro leaves. Shake the pan and simmer for 5 minutes more. Then, switch off the heat and let the mixture stand for 2 to 3 minutes before serving.

GOAN SHRIMP CURRY

Serves 4

Some of the most delicious spiced dishes are also the simplest. Experiment with the proportions in the spice mix to find the flavor you like most.

INGREDIENTS

3 to 4 whole dried chiles

¼ tsp black peppercorns

½ tsp cumin seeds

1 tsp coriander seeds

2 tbsp grated fresh coconut or shredded coconut

4 to 5 garlic cloves, chopped

2 tbsp oil

1 onion, finely chopped

2 tsp grated fresh gingerroot

1 to 2 fresh green chiles

1 tsp salt

¾ cup water

2 tbsp tamarind pulp or 1 tbsp vinegar

1 lb shelled small shrimp

2 tomatoes

2 tbsp freshly chopped cilantro

few cooked shrimp in shells, for the garnish

Crumble the whole dried chiles into a mortar. Add the peppercorns and cumin and coriander seeds and pound with a pestle. Then add the coconut and garlic and pound the mixture again, to make a paste.

Heat the oil in a saucepan and fry the onion over low heat. As it begins to turn translucent, add the ginger and green chiles and cook for 30 seconds. Stir in the spice paste, with the salt, and fry for about 1 minute, adding a little of the water if necessary, to thin the mixture.

Add the tamarind pulp or vinegar and stir continuously for 30 seconds.

COOK'S TIP

You can use a coffee grinder to make the paste, but it is best to keep it for spices thereafter, unless you like very spicy coffee!

Stir in the shrimp and tomatoes until both are coated in the sauce. Add the remaining water and let the curry cook for 5 minutes over a medium heat.

Add most of the cilantro leaves and simmer for 5 to 7 minutes more. Garnish with the remaining cilantro leaves and the whole shrimp.

STIR-FRIED SQUID WITH CHILES AND VEGETABLES

Serves 3 to 4

This is a Korean recipe, and to be truly authentic, you should use the hot, fermented bean paste, *kochujang*, and Korea's excellent coarsely pounded red chili powder. Korean chili powder adds a characteristic bright, carmine pink color. A mixture of cayenne pepper and paprika will give a similar result. Chili bean paste can be substituted for the *kochujang*.

INGREDIENTS

1¼ lb cleaned squid

3 tbsp vegetable oil

1 onion, thinly sliced

2 garlic cloves, minced

1 carrot, thinly sliced lengthwise

1 zucchini, thinly sliced lengthwise

2 to 3 long fresh red chiles, thinly sliced lengthwise

2 long fresh green chiles, thinly sliced lengthwise

1 tbsp *kochujang* or chili bean paste

about ½ tsp Korean chili powder, or cayenne pepper mixed with paprika

1 tsp sugar

salt and pepper

2 scallions, white and green parts sliced diagonally

2 tsp sesame oil

toasted sesame seeds, for the garnish

Prepare the squid as described in the recipe for Squid with Hot Pepper Sauce on page 67. Cut open each squid body so that it lies flat, then cut across into 2½- by ½-inch pieces. Cut the tentacles into 2½-inch lengths.

Bring a large saucepan of water to a boil. Add all the squid simultaneously and take the pan off the heat. Stir immediately and continue to stir for about 40 seconds, until the squid turns white. Drain well and discard the water.

Heat the oil in a large skillet over a moderate heat. Add the onion, garlic, and carrot. Stir for 30 to 40 seconds, then add the zucchini and chiles. Stir in 2 tsp *kochujang* or chili bean paste, with half the chili powder or cayenne mixture. Stir for 30 seconds. Stir in the squid with the remaining *kochujang* and chili powder or cayenne mixture. Add the sugar and season with the salt and pepper. Cook over a low heat for 2 minutes, then add the scallions and sesame oil. Tip into a warm serving dish and garnish with the toasted sesame seeds.

HOT CHILE

MIXED FISH, CREOLE STYLE

Serves 4

Not surprisingly, chiles and bell peppers are great companions. Try them in this quick and tasty fish dish.

INGREDIENTS

2 tbsp oil

1 large onion, chopped

2 garlic cloves, minced

4 to 5 rocotillo chiles, seeded

2 celery stalks, chopped

1 red bell pepper, seeded and sliced

1 green bell pepper, seeded and sliced

2 tbsp tomato paste

2 tbsp water

1¼ cups fish or chicken stock

14-oz can crushed tomatoes

1 tsp Worcestershire sauce

salt and pepper

8 oz white fish fillets, such as cod

8 oz mackerel fillets

1 tbsp freshly chopped oregano

1 tbsp freshly chopped marjoram

juice of ½ lime

4 oz shelled raw shrimp

sprigs of fresh oregano or marjoram, for the garnish

Heat the oil in a large pan and sauté the onion, garlic, chiles, and celery for 5 minutes. Add the peppers and cook for 3 minutes more.

Mix the tomato paste with the water and stir into the pan with the stock, crushed tomatoes, and Worcestershire sauce. Add salt and pepper to taste. Bring to a boil, then reduce the heat and simmer for about 20 minutes, or until the sauce has reduced and is thick.

Skin the fish fillets and discard any bones. Cut the fish into bite-size pieces. Rinse and pat dry with paper towels.

Add the fish to the pan with the herbs and lime juice. Simmer for 6 minutes more. Add the shrimp and cook for 4 minutes more and flakes easily when tested with the point of a knife.

Garnish with the herbs and serve.

SEAFOOD GUMBO

Serves 4

Gumbos vary from region to region; there are no hard and fast rules. One of the staple ingredients is okra, which gives the dish its characteristic texture. The filé powder is used as a thickening agent; flour can be used instead.

INGREDIENTS

2 tbsp corn or sunflower oil

1 large onion, chopped

2 garlic cloves, crushed

2–3 Jamaican hot chiles, seeded and chopped

2 celery stalks, chopped

2 red bell peppers, seeded and sliced

4 oz slab bacon, chopped

2 tbsp filé powder or flour

3 smoked pork sausages or Italian sausages, cut into chunks

1½ cups peeled and chopped tomatoes

1½ cups trimmed and sliced okra

2½ cups chicken stock

8 oz monkfish, central bone and skin removed and cubed

8 oz raw shrimp, shelled and deveined

8 oz squid, prepared (page 67) and sliced

½ to 1 tsp hot pepper sauce

salt and pepper

1 cup freshly cooked long-grain rice

2 tbsp freshly chopped parsley

Heat the oil in a large pan and gently sauté the onion, garlic, chiles, and celery for 5 minutes, or until soft.

Add the sliced red bell peppers and the bacon, and sauté for 3 minutes more. Sprinkle in the filé powder or flour and cook gently for a further 3 minutes.

Add the sausages, tomatoes, okra, and stock, then bring to a boil. Reduce the heat and simmer for 10 minutes, stirring occasionally. Add the monkfish and simmer for 10 minutes more, or until the fish is almost tender.

Stir in the shrimp, squid, and hot pepper sauce, with salt and pepper to taste. Cook for 5 to 7 minutes, or until all the fish is cooked through and flakes easily, when tested with the tip of a knife. Take care not to overcook the squid. Finally add the rice and parsley. Heat through for 5 to 7 minutes and serve.

COOK'S TIP
Use a 10-oz package of frozen sliced okra instead of fresh, if you like. It will not be necessary to thaw it before adding to the pan.

CHICKEN AND CHILES IN SOUR CREAM SAUCE

Serves 4

This is a versatile recipe. You can serve it for a simple supper, with taco chips or hot toast, or dress it up for company by surrounding it with crescents of cooked puff pastry and accompanying it with snow peas and baby carrots.

INGREDIENTS

4 fresh poblano chiles

2 to 3 tbsp lard or olive oil

1 large red onion, chopped

1 lb cooked chicken meat, shredded

1 cup sour cream

1 cup shredded Cheddar or Monterey Jack cheese

salt and pepper

fresh cilantro or parsley, for the garnish

Preheat the broiler. Broil the chiles, turning occasionally, until they are blistered all over. Put them in a bowl, cover with paper towels and set aside while you cook the onion.

Heat the lard or oil in a skillet and sauté the onion for 5 to 7 minutes, until translucent. Peel the chiles, slit them open and remove the seeds and veins. Dice the flesh finely.

Add the chicken and the chiles to the onion. Stir over the heat for about 5 minutes, until both are warm.

Add the sour cream and the shredded cheese, with salt and pepper to taste. Stir continuously over low heat for 2 or 3 minutes, until the cheese melts.

Transfer to a warmed serving dish. Garnish with cilantro or parsley and serve immediately.

COOK'S TIP

To make puff pastry crescents, cut circles of puff pastry using a round cutter, then move the cutter across and cut again to make crescents. Brush the crescents with beaten egg and bake in a preheated 400°F oven for about 10 minutes, until golden.

JAMAICAN CHICKEN

Serves 4 to 6

This Caribbean dish incorporates a classic rub – a combination of spices, brown sugar, and hot chile peppers that is applied to the chicken to enliven the dish.

INGREDIENTS

¼ cup chopped seeded fresh red chiles

4 tsp crushed allspice berries or 1 tsp ground allspice

6 garlic cloves, minced

2 tbsp peeled and chopped fresh gingerroot

2 tbsp soft dark brown sugar

¼ cup yellow mustard

1 tsp ground cinnamon

hot pepper sauce, to taste

½ cup olive oil

2 green onions, sliced

¼ cup cider vinegar

2 tbsp lime juice

salt and pepper

3 to 3½ lb chicken, jointed, or 6 large whole legs, or 4 large breasts

Purée the chiles in a blender or food processor. Add the allspice, garlic, ginger, sugar, mustard, cinnamon, hot pepper sauce, olive oil, green onions, vinegar, and lime juice. Process until the mixture forms a smooth paste. Add salt and pepper to taste and blend again.

Cut the chicken legs and thighs apart. Cut breasts in half crosswise, leaving the wings attached. Gently lift the skin up from the chicken, exposing the meat, and rub the paste underneath. Then rub into the outside of the skin. Place the pieces on a platter, cover with plastic wrap and refrigerate for 2 hours.

Barbecue or broil the chicken for about 40 minutes at low heat, turning once, until the paste on the skin has formed a dark brown crust. Alternatively, bake the chicken in a preheated 350°F oven for 50 minutes then transfer to the broiler and broil for 2–3 minutes on each side until the skin is dark brown and the paste has formed a crust.

STIR-FRIED CHICKEN

Serves 4

Stir-fries are perennially popular. This one mixes scallions and dried mushrooms with chiles and peppers.

INGREDIENTS

1 lb skinless, boneless chicken breasts, cut into strips

2 tbsp soy sauce

1 tbsp sugar

2 scallions, white and some green parts, finely chopped

2 to 3 fresh green chiles, seeded and minced

1-inch piece of fresh gingerroot, peeled and finely chopped

1½ tsp crushed toasted sesame seeds

freshly ground black pepper

1 small carrot, thinly sliced diagonally

3 dried Chinese black mushrooms, soaked for 30 minutes in hot water

1½ tbsp sesame oil

1 red bell pepper, seeded and cut into thin strips

FRIED EGG STRIP GARNISH

vegetable oil, for frying

1 egg, lightly beaten

Spread out the chicken strips in a shallow bowl. In a separate bowl, mix the soy sauce, sugar, scallions, chiles, ginger, sesame seeds, and plenty of pepper. Pour over the chicken, turning to coat the strips. Cover and let stand for 30 minutes.

Meanwhile, bring a small pan of water to a boil and cook the carrot slices for 5 minutes. Drain and set aside.

Drain the mushrooms. Cut out and discard any hard patches and the stalks. Slice the mushrooms caps.

Make the garnish. Heat a thin film of oil in a large nonstick skillet. Add the beaten egg, tilting the pan so that it forms a thin, even layer. Fry the omelet for 1 to 2 minutes until set, then flip over and fry the other side. Slide the omelet onto a board, roll it up and cut it into thin strips. Set aside.

Heat the sesame oil in a skillet. Drain the chicken, reserving the marinade and add it to the pan. Stir-fry for 2 to 3 minutes. Lift out of the pan and set aside. Add the mushrooms and carrots to the oil remaining in the pan and stir-fry for 2 minutes, then add the pepper and stir-fry for 1 minute more.

Return the chicken to the pan. Add the reserved marinade and bring to a boil. Stir and cook for 1 minute, then serve garnished with egg strips.

CHILE CHICKEN WITH PINE NUTS

Serves 4

INGREDIENTS

1 tbsp sunflower oil

1 tbsp butter

4 chicken portions

4 oz lean slab bacon, trimmed and cubed

1 onion, sliced

1 garlic clove, crushed

4 green fresno chiles, seeded and sliced

¼ cup all-purpose flour

2 cups chicken stock

grated peel of 1 lemon

salt and pepper

⅔ cup whole-kernel corn

2 tbsp freshly chopped parsley

3 tbsp pine nuts, toasted

Preheat the oven to 375°F. Heat the oil and butter in a skillet and seal the chicken portions and bacon cubes on all sides. Drain and place in a large ovenproof casserole.

Add the onion, garlic, and chiles to the skillet and gently sauté for 5 minutes, or until softened. Sprinkle in the flour and cook, stirring constantly, for 2 minutes. Gradually add the stock, then bring to a boil. Add the lemon peel with salt and pepper to taste.

Pour the onion mixture over the chicken and bacon, cover the casserole and cook for 40 minutes. Remove from the oven and stir in the corn. Cook for 15 minutes more or until the chicken portions are cooked through. Stir in the parsley and pine nuts, and serve.

CHICKEN KABOBS WITH CHILI SAUCE

Serves 4

Marinated chicken strips, threaded on wooden skewers and broiled, taste absolutely delicious with a chili and peanut sauce.

INGREDIENTS

10 oz skinless, boneless chicken breast, skinned

MARINADE

2 shallots, finely chopped

1 garlic clove, crushed

4 Thai red chiles, seeded and chopped

2-inch piece gingerroot, peeled and grated

2 tbsp soy sauce

2 tsp honey, warmed

2 tbsp lemon juice

chopped chile, for the garnish

CHILI SAUCE

1 Thai red chile, seeded and finely chopped

1 tbsp lime juice

¼ cup Thai fish sauce

1 tbsp roasted peanuts, finely crushed

2 scallions, trimmed and finely shredded

If using wooden skewers, soak them in cold water for 1 hour so that they do not scorch under the broiler.

Cut the chicken breasts into narrow 3- x ½-inch strips, and place in a shallow dish. Combine all the marinade ingredients in a bowl and pour over the chicken strips. Turn to ensure they are well coated. Cover the dish and chill for at least 3 hours, turning the chicken occasionally in the marinade.

Meanwhile, prepare the chili sauce. Mix all the ingredients into a small pan and heat through, stirring occasionally. Keep hot until required.

Preheat the broiler to medium-high. Drain the chicken, reserving the marinade, and thread onto the drained wooden skewers.

Brush the chicken strips with a little of the reserved marinade and broil for 8 to 10 minutes, brushing occasionally with more marinade and turning the kabobs several times, until the chicken is cooked. Garnish with the chopped chile and serve with the sauce.

ARROZ CON POLLO

Serves 4

The title simply means rice with chicken, but the reality is considerably more exciting. In Mexico, where the dish is extremely popular, chiles add a fiery note, and the dish resembles a spicy paella.

INGREDIENTS

3 tbsp olive or sunflower oil

4 chicken portions, cut in half

1 Spanish onion, chopped

2 garlic cloves, crushed

5 red Anaheim chiles, seeded and sliced

2 cups risotto rice

few strands of saffron

2½ to 3¾ cups chicken stock

salt and pepper

4 oz raw shelled shrimp

⅔ cup shelled peas

⅔ cup cut green beans

1 lb fresh mussels, scrubbed, beards removed and any open ones discarded

lemon wedges and flat-leafed parsley, for the garnish

Heat the oil in a paella or large skillet and brown the chicken on all sides. Lift out of the pan and drain on paper towels.

Add the onion, garlic, and chiles to the oil remaining in the pan and sauté for 5 minutes. Stir in the rice and saffron. Cook, stirring occasionally, for 3 minutes more.

Return the chicken to the pan and stir in 2 cups of the stock, with salt and pepper to taste. Bring to a boil, then lower the heat and simmer for 20 minutes, adding more stock as necessary.

Add the shrimp, vegetables, and mussels to the pan with extra stock if required. Cook for 8 to 10 minutes

more, or until the rice is tender and the chicken is cooked. Discard any mussels that have not opened. Check the seasoning, garnish with the lemon wedges and parsley, and serve.

SPATCHCOCKED CHICKEN WITH CHILI SAUCE

Serves 4

Spatchcock the chicken by placing it breast down and splitting it in half with cleaver, without cutting clear through to the breast. Open the carcass out, turn it over and flatten it.

INGREDIENTS

3 lb whole chicken, spatchcocked

10 garlic cloves, finely chopped

2 tbsp black peppercorns, crushed

2 tbsp light soy sauce

2 tbsp sugar

2 tbsp brandy

1 tsp salt

tomato peel roses and lettuce leaves, for the garnish

SAUCE

1 cup white vinegar

½ cup sugar

3 garlic cloves, roughly chopped

2 fresh red chiles, pounded well

½ tbsp salt

Mix the garlic, peppercorns, soy sauce, sugar, brandy, and salt in a dish that will hold the flattened chicken. Add the bird, spoon the marinade over and marinate for 3 to 4 hours. Preheat the oven to 350°F. Put the chicken in a roasting tin, brush with a little of the marinade and roast for 40 minutes, turning the bird halfway through. Meanwhile, mix all the sauce ingredients in a pan and boil until thick. Cool.

Garnish the chicken with roses shaped from pared tomato peel, and lettuce leaves. Serve with the sauce.

CHILI-TEQUILA CHICKEN WINGS

Serves 4

Chili spices season the chicken wings while tequila and citrus juices tenderize them. These are delicious served on their own or with other barbecued foods.

INGREDIENTS

3 dried chipotle chiles

5 garlic cloves, chopped

juice of 2 limes

juice of 1 orange

2 tbsp tequila

1 tbsp mild chili powder

2 tbsp vegetable oil

1 tsp sugar

¼ tsp ground allspice

pinch of ground cinnamon

pinch of ground cumin

pinch of dried oregano, crumbled

salt and pepper

12 to 16 chicken wings

Roast the dried chipotle chiles in a nonstick skillet for 2 to 3 minutes, taking care not to let them scorch. Tip into a bowl and add hot (not boiling) water. Soak for at least 10 minutes until soft, then purée in a blender or using a mortar and pestle.

In a large shallow dish, mix the chiles with all the remaining ingredients except the chicken. Season well.

Add the chicken wings and turn to coat them in the mixture. Cover and marinate for at least 3 hours, preferably overnight.

Grill over medium coals for 15 to 20 minutes or until the wings are crisply browned and cooked through.

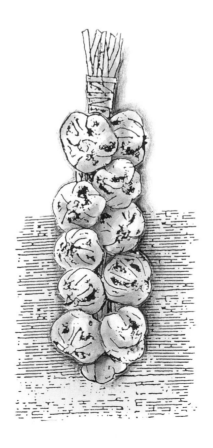

BARBECUED CHICKEN WINGS

Serves 4

Everyone's favorite – barbecued chicken wings are so good that it makes sense to cook double the quantity.

INGREDIENTS

12 to 16 chicken wings

Green Chili Sauce (page 174), tossed green salad and warm bread, to serve

MARINADE

2 tbsp sunflower oil

2 tbsp soft dark brown sugar

2 tbsp soy sauce

½ cup orange juice

2 garlic cloves, crushed

4 red jalapeño chiles, seeded and sliced

Wipe the chicken wings and trim them if necessary. Place in a single layer in a large, shallow dish.

Mix all the marinade ingredients together in a pan and heat through, stirring occasionally, until the sugar has dissolved. Bring to a boil and boil for 5 minutes. Let cool slightly, then pour over the chicken wings. Turn the wings to ensure they are well coated, then cover the dish and leave in a cool place for at least 3 hours. Turn the wings or spoon the marinade over the chicken occasionally.

If you plan to use wooden skewers to hold the wings, soak them in cold water for 1 hour so that they do not scorch on the barbecue.

Drain the chicken wings, reserving a little of the marinade, and thread onto the drained skewers. Place on the barbecue grill and brush with the reserved marinade. Cook over medium coals for 15 to 20 minutes, turning occasionally and brushing with the reserved marinade, until the wings are cooked. Serve with the chili sauce, salad, and bread.

SPICED CHICKEN WITH GREEN PEPPER

Serves 4

This simple stir-fry owes its superb flavor to the combination of sauces added at the end.

INGREDIENTS

¼ cup corn oil

I tbsp chopped garlic

11 oz skinless, boneless chicken
breasts, cut lengthwise into ½-inch
slices

I cup sliced green pepper

5 fresh red chiles, sliced lengthwise

I onion, thickly sliced

I tbsp oyster sauce

½ tbsp light soy sauce

I tsp fish sauce

¼ tsp dark soy sauce

½ cup basil leaves

cooked rice, for serving

Heat the oil in a wok or pan, add the garlic and chicken and fry well for I minute. Add the green pepper and chiles, mix, then add the onion and cook for I minute. One by one stir in the sauces, cooking for about 30 seconds after each addition. Check that the chicken is cooked through, then stir in the basil. Remove from the heat immediately after stirring in the basil and serve the stir-fry with rice.

COOK'S TIP

It is a good idea to preheat a wok for a few seconds before adding any oil for stir-frying. Add the oil in an even drizzle around the top of the wok – bracelet-style – so that it slides down to coat the entire inner surface. You do not need to use much oil. Give it a few seconds to heat before adding the food.

CHICKEN WITH CHICK-PEAS

Serves 4

Chick-peas – or garbanzos, as they are also known – make a wonderful addition to spiced dishes. If you use dried chick-peas, rather than canned, soak them in water overnight and cook them for 1½ to 2 hours, until tender, before adding them to the pan.

INGREDIENTS

1 lb skinless, boneless chicken breasts, cut into 1-inch cubes

1 onion, chopped

2 tomatoes, 1 chopped, 1 sliced

1 garlic clove, minced

2 tsp minced fresh gingerroot, plus 1 tsp fresh gingerroot cut into very fine matchstick strips

1 tsp salt

1 tsp chili powder

¼ tsp turmeric

½ tsp garam masala

1 tbsp oil

1½ cups drained canned chick-peas (garbanzos)

about 1 cup water

1 to 2 fresh green chiles

½ tsp cumin seeds, crushed

3 tbsp freshly chopped cilantro leaves, or chopped scallions for the garnish

2 tsp lemon juice

Put the chicken into a heavy saucepan. Add the onion and the chopped tomato, then stir in the garlic and the minced ginger. Sprinkle over the salt. Cook over a low heat for 10 minutes or until the chicken releases its moisture, stirring occasionally.

Add the chili powder, turmeric, and garam masala and cook for 10 to 15 minutes more.

Add the oil and cook the mixture uncovered until almost all the moisture has evaporated and the chicken and vegetables look slightly glazed.

Add the chick-peas and green chiles. Mix them in well, then add the water. Bring it to a boil then lower the heat and simmer for 7 to 8 minutes.

Lastly, add the cumin seeds, ginger strips, cilantro, and lemon juice. Simmer for a couple more minutes, then garnish the dish with tomato slices, cilantro or chopped scallions.

CHICKEN IN RED CHILI AND TOMATO SAUCE

Serves 4

As colorful as it is good to eat, this is sure to prove popular with family and friends.

INGREDIENTS

6 dried ancho chiles, roasted

2½ lb chicken

2 onions

1 carrot, roughly chopped

3 bay leaves

2 garlic cloves

4 tbsp sesame seeds, toasted

½ tsp ground cinnamon

½ tsp ground cloves

1 tbsp sunflower oil

14-oz can crushed tomatoes

1 tbsp tomato paste

1 tbsp freshly chopped oregano

salad and warm bread, to serve

Rehydrate the roasted chiles by soaking them in hot water for 10 minutes. Place the chicken in a large pan with one of the onions, the carrot, and the bay leaves. Cover with cold water and bring to a boil. Skim off any foam that rises to the surface. Cover the pan with a lid and simmer for 1½ hours, or until the chicken is tender and fully cooked.

Let the chicken cool, then remove the cooked chicken meat from the carcass, discarding the skin, and cut into thin strips. Reserve 1¼ cups of the cooking liquid.

Drain the chiles and put them in a food processor. Chop the remaining onion and add it to the chiles with the garlic, sesame seeds, and spices. Process with a little of the reserved stock to make a smooth paste.

Heat the oil in a skillet and cook the paste gently for 2 minutes. Add the chopped tomatoes, tomato paste, and remaining stock. Bring to a boil, reduce the heat and simmer for 10 minutes.

Add the chicken to the pan and simmer for 10 to 15 minutes more, or until the chicken is piping hot. Sprinkle with the chopped oregano and serve.

VIETNAMESE BROILED CHICKEN

Serves 4

If preferred, bird's eye (Thai) chiles can be substituted for the dried chiles. Depending on your heat tolerance, you should use 1 to 3 bird's eye (Thai) chiles instead of the dried ancho chiles.

INGREDIENTS

6 dried ancho chiles, roasted and seeded

2 lemongrass stalks, outer leaves removed and chopped

2 garlic cloves, crushed

2-inch piece gingerroot, peeled and grated

1 cup chopped onions

1 tbsp soft dark brown sugar

1 tsp turmeric

2 tbsp sunflower oil

4 chicken portions, cut in half

flat-leafed parsley, lemon wedges, and sliced green chiles, for the garnish

Rehydrate the roasted chiles by soaking them in hot water for 10 minutes. Drain, then put the chiles into a food processor with the lemongrass, garlic, ginger, onions, sugar, and turmeric. Blend to form a thick, chunky paste.

Heat the oil in a skillet and cook the paste, stirring constantly, for 2 minutes. Remove from the heat, let cool slightly and brush over the chicken portions. Cover the chicken and leave in a cool place for at least 3 hours.

Preheat the broiler to medium-high. Place the chicken on the broiler rack lined with foil and broil, turning occasionally, for 15 minutes, or until the chicken is tender and the juices run clear. Serve garnished with flat-leafed parsley, lemon wedges, and slices of green chiles.

MARINATED BROILED CHICKEN

Serves 4

Probably better known as Chicken Tikka, this is one of the most popular choices on Indian restaurant menus. It is easy to make, and when prepared by the method below, it is a low-fat dish.

INGREDIENTS

4 skinless, boneless chicken breasts

1 large onion, chopped

2 garlic cloves, minced

1 tbsp minced fresh gingerroot

2 fresh green chiles, roughly chopped

2 tbsp plain yogurt

½ to 1 tsp chili powder

½ tsp garam masala

¼ tsp ground mace

1 tbsp lemon juice

freshly chopped cilantro

½ tsp salt

Score the chicken breasts diagonally across in 3 to 4 places.

Combine the remaining ingredients in a blender or food processor and process to a smooth paste. Spread the spice paste over the chicken pieces, rubbing it in well. Cover the chicken and refrigerate for at least 3 hours, preferably overnight.

Preheat the broiler to high and line the broiler pan with foil. Broil the chicken breasts under the hot broiler for 4 to 5 minutes, then reduce the heat and continue cooking for another 15 to 20 minutes, turning them over halfway through.

CHICKEN FRIED WITH CASHEW NUTS

Serves 4

Chicken and cashews are a timeless combination. Chiles give the dish a bit of zip.

INGREDIENTS

11 oz skinless, boneless chicken breasts, cut into slices

flour for coating

1 cup corn oil

4 dried red chiles, fried and cut into ½-inch pieces

1 tbsp chopped garlic

10 scallions, white parts only, cut into 2-inch pieces

⅓ cup unsalted cashew nuts, roasted

1 onion, sliced

2 tbsp oyster sauce

1 tbsp light soy sauce

dash of dark soy sauce

1 tbsp sugar

Coat the chicken breasts lightly with flour. The easiest way to do this is to put the flour in a strong plastic bag and add the chicken slices. Shake the bag until the slices are evenly coated, then lift them out, leaving the excess flour behind. Heat the oil in a pan or wok and stir-fry the chicken for about 5 minutes until light brown. Remove almost all the oil from the pan.

Add the chiles and garlic to the chicken in the pan and fry for 1 minute. Add the scallions, cashews, and onion and stir-fry for 3 minutes.

Stir in the sauces and sugar and cook for 1 or 2 minutes, until the chicken and vegetables are glazed. Serve immediately.

COOK'S TIP

If you prefer a milder chili flavor, leave the chiles whole and either remove them before serving or give guests the choice of whether to leave them in or take them out.

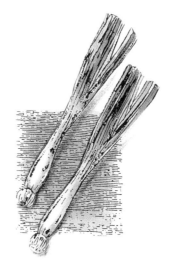

DUCK IN GREEN CHILI SAUCE

Serves 4

Arrowroot is used to thicken the sauce without muddying the color, but cornstarch can be used instead.

INGREDIENTS

4 green serrano chiles, seeded and sliced

1½ cups seeded and chopped tomatillos or green tomatoes

1 onion, chopped

2 garlic cloves, chopped

grated peel of ½ lemon, if using green tomatoes

⅔ cup chicken stock

2 tbsp freshly chopped cilantro

2 tsp honey

salt and pepper

1 tbsp arrowroot

1 tbsp water

4 duck breasts

Red Chili Sauce (page 175) for serving

cilantro sprigs, for the garnish

Preheat the broiler to medium-high. Put the chiles, tomatillos or tomatoes, garlic, and lemon peel, if using, into a food processor. Process to a purée, then press through a fine strainer into a pan. Gradually stir in the stock.

Heat the chili mixture gently for 4 minutes, stirring occasionally. Stir in the cilantro and honey, with salt and pepper to taste.

Mix the arrowroot with the water, stir into the pan and cook, stirring constantly, until the sauce thickens and clears. Keep warm.

Wipe the duck breasts, discard any excess fat and prick the skin with a fork. Season with salt and pepper.

Place the duck breasts, skin side up, in a broiler pan. Broil, turning at least once, for 25 minutes, or until cooked to personal preference.

To serve, pour a little of the chili sauce onto each serving plate. Slice the duck breasts. Arrange in a fan shape with the chili sauce and serve extra sauce separately. Garnish with cilantro sprigs.

DUCK BREASTS WITH PUMPKIN SEEDS

Serves 4

The pumpkin seeds in the chili sauce are used to thicken and flavor. Mexican cooks also use sesame seeds and pine nuts for the same purpose.

INGREDIENTS

4 duck breasts, about 6 oz each

SAUCE

⅓ cup pumpkin seeds, toasted

2 tbsp sunflower oil

1 small onion, chopped

3 or 4 green fresno chiles, seeded and chopped

2 garlic cloves, chopped

⅔ cup chicken stock

1 tbsp freshly chopped cilantro

¼ tsp salt

2 cups chopped fresh spinach

Make the sauce. Reserve a few of the pumpkin seeds for the garnish; finely grind the remainder.

Heat the oil in a pan and gently sauté the onion, chiles, and garlic for 3 minutes. Add the stock and simmer for 1 minute. Stir in the ground pumpkin seeds, cilantro, salt, and spinach and simmer for 3 minutes more. Remove from the heat and keep warm.

Preheat the broiler to high and line the broiler pan with foil.

Prick the skin on the duck breasts with a fork and place, skin-side uppermost, in the broiler pan. Broil for 2 minutes, on each side, then reduce the temperature of the broiler to medium-hot and turn the duck breasts over. Continue broiling for 15 to 20 minutes, turning at least once, until the duck is cooked to personal preference. Serve the duck breasts, sprinkled with the reserved pumpkin seeds. Hand the sauce separately.

DUCK WITH TWO SAUCES

Serves 4

A very popular dish, of Chinese origin, with two contrasting sauces.

INGREDIENTS	COOKED SAUCE	SOY CHILI SAUCE
4 lb roasting duck	2 cups chicken stock	½ cup dark soy sauce
red food coloring	1 tbsp sugar	3 fresh red chiles, sliced thinly into circles
4 cups hot boiled rice	½ tbsp light soy sauce	
4 tbsp thinly sliced pickled ginger	1 tsp dark soy sauce	1 tbsp sugar
4 tbsp thinly sliced sweet dill pickle	1 tsp flour	½ tbsp vinegar

Preheat the oven to 400°F. Wipe the duck, inside and out, discarding any excess fat from the cavity. Prick the skin all over with a fork, then rub it with red food coloring. Roast the duck on a rack over a roasting pan for 1¾ to 2 hours, until fully cooked. Remove the flesh and cut it into 2½- x ½-inch slices. Keep hot.

Heat the ingredients for the cooked sauce together in a pan and boil for 1 minute. Mix the ingredients for the soy chili sauce in a bowl.

Divide the rice among four serving plates, and arrange the duck meat over the top. Spoon the cooked sauce over and garnish with the ginger and pickle slices. Hand the soy chili sauce separately.

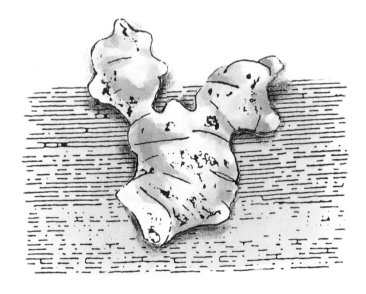

ROAST DUCK WITH CHILES

Serves 4

Roast duck with a chili rub makes an unusual dish, especially when served with the spicy salsa.

INGREDIENTS

4 lb roasting duck

4 red serrano chiles, seeded and finely chopped

2 tbsp soft dark brown sugar

1 tsp salt

1 tsp ground cinnamon

½ tsp ground cloves

grated peel of 1 lime

grated lime peel and flat-leafed parsley, for the garnish

SALSA

1½ cups peeled, seeded and finely chopped ripe tomatoes

6 scallions, finely chopped

1 passion fruit (granadilla) halved, with the seeds removed

2 red serrano chiles, seeded and finely chopped

Wipe the duck, inside and out, discarding any excess fat from the cavity. Prick the skin all over with a fork. Mix the chiles, sugar, salt, cinnamon, cloves, and lime peel in a bowl. Sprinkle the inside of the duck with 1 tbsp of the mixture and use the remainder to rub all over the duck skin. Leave in a cool place for at least 4 hours.

Make the Salsa. Combine all the ingredients in a bowl. Set aside to let the flavors develop.

At least 15 minutes before roasting the duck, preheat the oven to 400°F.

Place the duck on a trivet or rack standing in a roasting pan. Roast for 1¾ to 2 hours, or until the duck is tender and the juices run clear when the thickest part of a thigh is pierced with a skewer.

Garnish the cooked duck with lime peel and flat-leafed parsley, and serve with the salsa.

WHITE CHILI WITH CHICKEN

Serves 6

This is a low-fat, moderately spicy chili, made with chicken, white beans, and Anaheim chiles.

INGREDIENTS

2 cups white beans, picked over and soaked overnight

1 tbsp chili powder

½ tsp ground cumin

½ tsp dried thyme

½ tsp dried oregano

½ tsp cayenne pepper

½ tsp garlic powder

1 tbsp flour

3 boneless, skinless chicken breasts, cut into ½-inch cubes

2 tbsp vegetable oil

1 onion, chopped

1 celery stalk, chopped

2 cups chicken stock

4 Anaheim chiles, roasted, peeled and chopped, or 4-oz can chopped green chiles

about 1 tsp salt

¼ cup freshly chopped cilantro

Drain the beans, put them in a large pan and barely cover with fresh water. Bring to a boil, boil hard for 5 minutes, then reduce the heat to a simmer.

Mix the spices, herbs, seasonings, and flour in a strong plastic bag. Add the chicken cubes and toss until they are evenly coated with the spice mix. Set aside.

Heat 1 tablespoon of the oil in a skillet and sauté the onion and celery for 6 minutes. Add the vegetables to the beans.

Heat the remaining oil in the cleaned skillet and cook the chicken, turning often, until all sides are lightly browned. Add the chicken to the beans with the chicken stock and chiles. Simmer for about 1½ hours, until the beans are tender, adding water or chicken stock if the chili looks too dry. Add salt to taste. Sprinkle in the cilantro just before serving.

GROUND TURKEY CHILI WITH BLACK BEANS

Serves 4 to 6

Set your tastebuds sizzling with this hot and spicy chili.

INGREDIENTS

2 dried ancho chiles

2 dried Anaheim chiles

1 cup boiling water

1 lb ground turkey

1 cup chicken stock

2 tbsp vegetable oil

1 medium onion, chopped

1 celery stalk, chopped

2 fresh jalapeño or serrano chiles, unseeded, minced

14-oz can chopped tomatoes

¼ tsp dried sage

1 tsp dried oregano

15-oz can black beans

about 1 tsp salt

Cut the dried chiles in half and remove the stems and seeds. Put them in a small heatproof bowl. Pour the boiling water over the chiles, making sure all parts are immersed. Let chiles soak for about 30 minutes while you prepare the other ingredients.

Brown the ground turkey in a nonstick skillet, stirring to break up any large lumps. Drain fat, if needed. Put the turkey in a large saucepan and add the chicken stock. Bring to simmering point.

Heat the oil in the cleaned skillet and sauté the onion and celery for 5 minutes. Tip the contents of the skillet into the pan and add the fresh chiles, canned tomatoes, sage, and oregano. Bring to a boil, then lower the heat and let the turkey mixture simmer.

Pour the dried chiles and their soaking water into a blender or food processor. Purée until a thick red sauce forms. Strain the sauce to remove the seeds and bits of skin. Discard the solids. Add the sauce to the turkey mixture and simmer for 15 minutes, adding water or chicken stock if needed. Stir in the beans, with salt to taste. Heat through and serve.

TURKEY IN CHOCOLATE SAUCE

Serves 4

Don't be put off by the title – the only evidence of chocolate in this classic Mexican dish is in the richness of the sauce.

INGREDIENTS

3 dried ancho chiles

3 dried pasilla chiles

3 dried mulato chiles

1 onion, chopped

2 garlic cloves, minced

4 tbsp sesame seeds, toasted

2 tbsp flaked almonds, toasted

1 tsp ground coriander

½ tsp freshly ground black pepper

few cloves

3 to 4 tbsp sunflower oil

1¼ cups chicken stock

3 cups peeled, seeded and chopped tomatoes

2 tsp ground cinnamon

⅓ cup raisins

½ cup pumpkin seeds, toasted

2 oz unsweetened chocolate, melted

1 tbsp red wine vinegar

8 turkey thigh portions or 2 skinless, boneless chicken breasts

fresh herbs, for the garnish

Roast the dried chiles in a nonstick skillet for 2 to 3 minutes, taking care not to let them scorch. Tip into a bowl and add hot (not boiling) water. Soak for at least 10 minutes until soft, then drain, reserving the soaking liquid.

Put the rehydrated chiles in a food processor and add the onion, garlic, and half the sesame seeds, with the almonds, coriander, black pepper, and cloves. Grind to form a paste.

Heat 2 tbsp of the oil in a heavy pan and gently cook the paste for 5 minutes, stirring frequently.

Add ⅔ cup of the stock, the tomatoes, cinnamon, raisins, and pumpkin seeds. Bring to a boil, then reduce the heat and simmer for 15 minutes, or until a thick consistency is reached. Stir in the melted chocolate and vinegar, mixing well. Cover the pan and keep the mixture warm until needed.

Heat the remaining oil in a skillet and seal the turkey thighs or chicken breasts on all sides. Drain off the oil and add the remaining stock. Bring to a boil, then reduce the heat and simmer for 15 minutes, or until tender. Drain off any liquid.

Pour the sauce over the turkey or chicken and reheat gently. Sprinkle the remaining toasted sesame seeds over and garnish with fresh herbs.

COOK'S TIP
Use a mortar and pestle to make the chili paste if you prefer.

MEAT DISHES

BISTECK RANCHERO

Serves 4

This is a traditional Mexican way of cooking steak. As is often the case in Mexican cooking, the steak is served well done, having first been panfried and then smothered with vegetables and chiles and cooked in the covered skillet.

INGREDIENTS

1½ tbsp vegetable oil

1½ lb very thinly sliced beef steak

1 onion, thickly sliced

2 beefsteak tomatoes, chopped or sliced

2 green California chiles, seeded and sliced

3 to 4 serrano chiles, seeded and chopped

4 tbsp chicken stock

whole trimmed scallions, halved tomatoes and stuffed green olives, to garnish

Refried Beans (page 26) and side salad, for serving

Heat the oil in a large skillet. Pan-fry the steak over high heat for 2 minutes on each side. Smother with the onion slices, chopped tomatoes and chiles.

Pour over the stock, cover the skillet tightly and reduce the heat. Cook for about 15 minutes or until the steak is tender.

Garnish each portion with a scallion and half a tomato topped with a stuffed olive. Add a portion of refried beans to one side of the plate and a side salad to the other.

BEEF HOTPOT WITH CHILI MARINADE

Serves 4 to 6

In Korea, where this recipe originated, the hotpot is a communal one-pot meal prepared over a burner at the table. Everyone dips into the pot to select their chosen morsels. Any number of a wide variety of ingredients can be added, according to what is available, or to suit the occasion.

INGREDIENTS

1¼ lb sirloin or filet mignon, partly frozen

3 cups brown veal or chicken stock

6 celery stalks, cut into 2-inch pieces

2 young carrots, finely sliced diagonally

8 crimini mushrooms

8 scallions, cut diagonally into 2-inch pieces

6 Chinese leaves, cut into 2-inch pieces

1½ × 4-oz cakes of bean curd, cut into 1-inch cubes

MARINADE

2 tsp sesame seeds

3 tbsp sugar

1 fresh red chile, seeded and finely chopped

6 tbsp soy sauce

1 plump garlic clove, minced

COOK'S TIP

If you cook this in a fondue pot at the table, boil the stock in a saucepan before adding it to the seared meat.

Make the marinade. Heat a heavy nonstick skillet, add the sesame seeds and toast until pale brown. Remove and crush finely. Tip into a bowl and stir in the remaining marinade ingredients.

Slice the beef and cut into 1- × 2-inch strips. Put into a bowl. Pour over the marinade and stir to coat. Leave for 1 hour.

Heat a large heavy pan. Do not add any fat. Remove the beef from the marinade and add it to the pan.

Cook briefly to sear the meat all over, then lift it out with a slotted spoon. Set aside.

Add the stock and any remaining marinade to the pan and bring to a boil.

Add the celery and carrots to the pan. Boil for 5 minutes, then add the mushrooms, scallions, Chinese leaves, bean curd, and beef. Simmer together for 2 to 3 minutes, then place the pan over a burner and regulate the heat so that the stock simmers slowly while the hotpot is eaten.

COCONUT BEEF CURRY

Serves 8

This is one of the driest of Thai curries, and usually quite fiery. Use fewer chiles if you like.

INGREDIENTS

¼ cup corn oil

11 oz beef sirloin, cut into 1¼- x ¾- x ¼-inch pieces

3 cups thin coconut milk

1 tbsp Thai fish sauce

2 tsp sugar

2 fresh red chiles, sliced

2 kaffir lime leaves, finely sliced

⅓ cup basil leaves, for garnish

CURRY PASTE

6 dried red chiles, roughly chopped

7 white peppercorns

4 garlic cloves, roughly chopped

3 shallots, roughly chopped

2 freshly chopped cilantro stems

2 tsp salt

1 tsp grated fresh galangal or gingerroot

1 tsp roughly chopped lemongrass

1 tsp roughly chopped lime peel

1 tsp shrimp paste

Place all the curry paste ingredients in a mortar and pound with a pestle to form a paste. Alternatively, use a spice mill.

Heat the oil in a pan or wok and cook the curry paste for 3 to 4 minutes. Add the beef and stir-fry for 2 minutes, then add the coconut milk and cook over medium heat for about 15 minutes or until the beef is tender.

Add the fish sauce, sugar, lime leaves, and chiles. Transfer to a serving plate and sprinkle with the chopped lime peel and basil.

STIR-FRIED BEEF WITH GARLIC AND CHILES

Serves 3 to 4

Garlic and chiles give the character to this simple, tasty stir-fry, but the number of each can be adjusted according to personal taste.

INGREDIENTS

1 lb sirloin steak, cut into strips

2 tbsp soy sauce

1 scallion, white and green part thinly sliced

1½ tsp sesame oil

2 tbsp rice wine or dry sherry

1½ tsp sugar

1½ tbsp vegetable oil

3 garlic cloves, cut into slivers

4 fresh red chiles, seeded and cut into strips

Fried Egg Strip Garnish (see Stir-Fried Chicken, page 82), and toasted sesame seeds

Put the beef strips in a bowl. Add the soy sauce, scallion, sesame oil, rice wine or dry sherry, and sugar. Stir, then set aside to marinate for 1 hour.

Heat the oil in a skillet. Add the garlic and chiles, and stir-fry for about 1 minute over high heat until fragrant. Remove with a slotted spoon and reserve until later.

Lift the beef out of the marinade, and add the strips to the skillet. Stir-fry for 2 to 3 minutes. Return the chiles and garlic to the pan. Pour in the marinade and cook, stirring, over medium heat for about 2 minutes. Serve garnished with egg strips and toasted sesame seeds.

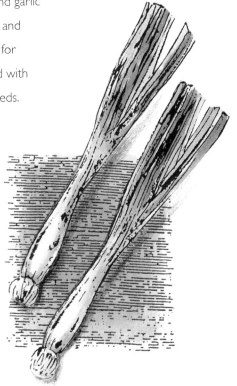

PICADILLO

Serves 4 to 6

A Mexican dish that can be made with chopped, ground, or thinly sliced beef. It is often used as a filling for tacos or bell peppers. The most authentic recipes call for chayote, a pear-shaped vegetable belonging to the gourd family. If you cannot get chayote, just leave it out.

INGREDIENTS

2 lb lean beef

4 tbsp olive oil

1 onion, chopped

2 to 4 garlic cloves, minced

1 chayote, peeled and cubed

1 large potato, peeled and cubed

2 beefsteak tomatoes, cut in chunks

2 carrots, sliced

1 zucchini, sliced

3 tbsp raisins

3 or more drained canned jalapeño chiles

10 pimiento-stuffed olives, halved

large pinch each of ground cinnamon and cloves

salt and pepper

1 cup shelled peas, thawed if frozen

½ cup flaked almonds, for the garnish

Cut the beef in ¼-inch wide strips, about 2 inches in length, or chop finely. Heat 3 tbsp of the oil in a heavy skillet and sauté the beef strips until browned. Add the onions and garlic and sauté for about 5 minutes, until golden.

Add all the other ingredients, except the peas and almonds. Bring to a boil, then reduce the heat and simmer for 20 to 30 minutes, depending on how well done you like the vegetables.

About 5 minutes before serving, stir in the peas. When they are tender and the picadillo is thick and flavorsome, spoon it into a serving dish and keep hot.

Heat the remaining olive oil in a small skillet and fry the almonds until golden. Sprinkle them over the picadillo and serve.

QUICK-COOK BEEF WITH BEAN CURD AND VEGETABLES

Serves 3 to 4

Richness and depth is given to the flavor of this spicy dish by making the stock with miso or *twoenjang*, Korean fermented bean curd. The beef is then cooked for just 2 minutes.

INGREDIENTS

8 oz sirloin or round steak, cut into 1- × 2-inch slices

2 tsp sesame oil

1½ tsp sugar

freshly ground black pepper

8 dried Chinese black mushrooms

1 onion, thinly sliced into rings

1 zucchini, sliced

2 scallions, white and green parts sliced

1 to 2 fresh red chiles, seeded and thickly sliced

2 × 4-oz cakes of medium-firm bean curd, cut into 1½-inch chunks

STOCK

8 tablespoons miso or *twoenjang* (fermented bean curd)

4 cups water

2 garlic cloves, lightly crushed

1 onion, cut into chunks

1 carrot, cut into chunks

3 scallions, white and green parts cut into 3-inch lengths

Make the stock. Put the miso or *twoenjang* in a strainer placed over a saucepan. Slowly pour through the water, pressing the *twoenjang* or miso with the back of a wooden spoon so it is all pushed through. Add the remaining stock ingredients and bring to a boil. Reduce the heat, cover and simmer slowly for 30 minutes.

Meanwhile, place the beef in a bowl and add the sesame oil, sugar, and plenty of black pepper. Stir well to coat the slices. Leave for 30 minutes. Soak the Chinese mushrooms in hot water in a separate bowl for the same length of time.

Strain the stock, squeezing out as much liquid from the vegetables as possible. Pour the stock back into the cleaned pan. Drain the mushrooms and remove the stalks. Add the mushroom caps to the stock with the onion, zucchini, scallions, and chiles. Bring to a boil, then reduce the heat and simmer for 2 minutes. Add the beef to the stock with the bean curd. Return to a boil, reduce the heat and simmer for 2 minutes. Serve immediately.

CURRIED GROUND LAMB WITH CAULIFLOWER

Serves 4

INGREDIENTS

3 to 4 whole dried chiles or 1 tsp chili powder	¼ tsp turmeric	1 tbsp grated fresh gingerroot
½ tsp cumin seeds	½ tsp garam masala	3 to 4 fat garlic cloves, minced
10 oz lean ground lamb or beef	1 tsp salt	2 to 3 tbsp freshly chopped cilantro
1 small onion, chopped	2 cups cauliflower flowerets	cilantro sprigs, for the garnish
	1 tomato, chopped	

Heat the oil in a heavy saucepan. Add the dried chiles (do not put the chili powder in at this stage if you are using it instead) and cumin seeds. Fry these for 30 seconds over medium heat, then add the ground lamb or beef and the onion, stirring continuously.

Add the chili powder now, if using, then stir in the turmeric, garam masala, and salt. Mix thoroughly. Cover the pan, reduce the heat and simmer for 20 to 25 minutes.

Add the cauliflower, tomato, ginger, garlic, and the green chiles. Cook over medium heat for 10 to 12 minutes. When the moisture has evaporated, stir in half the cilantro. Spoon into a serving dish and sprinkle over the rest of the cilantro. Garnish with the cilantro sprigs and serve.

SPICY MEATLOAF

Serves 4

This is an excellent party dish because it can be prepared beforehand, chilled a day or two ahead or frozen and then simply thawed and served cold or heated on the day.

INGREDIENTS

1 large onion, roughly chopped

2 tsp grated fresh gingerroot

2 fresh green chiles, roughly chopped

1 tbsp plain yogurt

2 to 3 plump garlic cloves

3 tbsp freshly chopped cilantro

8 oz lean ground lamb or beef

1 tbsp cornstarch

½ tsp chili powder

¼ tsp garam masala

small pinch of ground mace

2 tsp lemon juice

cucumber and carrot sticks, onion rings, and lemon slices, for the garnish

Preheat the oven to 425°F. Put the onion, ginger, green chiles, yogurt, garlic, and cilantro in a blender and process to a paste.

Put the ground lamb or beef into a bowl and add the paste. Add all the remaining ingredients, except the lemon juice.

Mix the meat thoroughly, kneading it for a couple of minutes to ensure that the herbs and spices are evenly and well distributed.

With moistened hands, press the mixture into a round or oblong loaf shape, making sure that the surface is smooth. Place the loaf in the center of a piece of foil large enough to cover it and let it stand for 20 to 30 minutes.

Wrap the loaf and stand it on a baking sheet. Bake for 20 minutes. Unfold the foil to reveal the top of the loaf, then bake it for 5 to 7 minutes more, until it is golden brown. Serve hot or cold.

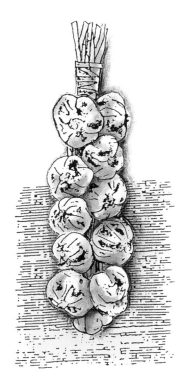

SCORCHER CHILI

Serves 4

This chili is for Texas purists – those who don't hold with beans or tomatoes in their chili and like it simple and scorching. The beer-based sauce gets its heat from pure *chile de arbol* powder and unseeded jalapeños, while pasilla and mild New Mexico or California pure chili powders fill out the chili flavor.

INGREDIENTS

2 tbsp vegetable oil

2 lb beef, cubed

1 onion, chopped

12-oz bottle of beer

2 beef bouillon cubes

3 jalapeño chiles, minced

1 tbsp pure pasilla chili powder

1 tbsp mild New Mexico or California chili powder

1 tsp *chile de arbol* powder

2 tsp ground cumin

2 tsp ground oregano

1 tsp garlic powder

1 tsp ground coriander

2 tbsp masa harina

3 tbsp cold water

about ½ tsp salt

Heat 1 tbsp of the oil in a skillet and cook the beef until browned. Remove the meat with a slotted spoon. Heat the remaining oil in the cleaned skillet and sauté the onion for 5 minutes.

Put the beef and sautéed onion in a large pan. Pour in the beef bouillon and bring to a boil. Add the remaining ingredients, except the masa harina and salt. Reduce the heat and simmer for at least 1½ hours until the meat is tender, adding water if needed.

Mix the masa harina to a paste with the water. Add to the chili and cook for 2 minutes. Stir in salt to taste, adjust the seasonings and serve.

SIMPLE BEEF AND SALSA CHILI

Serves 4

This chili is very easy to make, with bottled salsa providing the heart of the sauce. The spiciness will depend on the type of salsa you use, but can be increased by adding cayenne.

INGREDIENTS

2 tbsp vegetable oil

2 lb beef, cubed

1 onion, chopped

2 cups bottled red salsa, preferably chunky

8-oz can tomato sauce

2 beef bouillon cubes dissolved in 2 cups hot water

3 tbsp chili powder

1 tsp ground cumin

1 tsp dried oregano

cayenne pepper to taste

salt, if needed

Heat 1 tbsp of the oil in a skillet and cook the beef until lightly browned. Remove the meat with a slotted spoon. Heat the remaining oil in the cleaned skillet and sauté the onion for 5 minutes.

Put the beef, onion, salsa, and tomato sauce in a large saucepan. Add the beef bouillon, then stir in the chili powder, cumin, and oregano. Bring to a boil, reduce the heat and simmer for about 1½ hours until the meat is tender. Stir occasionally, adding water if needed. Taste and add cayenne and salt, if needed.

BEEF FAJITAS

Serves 4

Fajitas can be made from a poorer-quality cut of beef, in which case the meat is marinated in the piece for a longer period of time before being sliced across the grain and barbecued over a fierce heat. Fajitas should be served immediately, which is why many restaurants call this dish sizzling beef. For this recipe, a better quality of beef has been used but if you prefer, substitute chuck beef.

INGREDIENTS

1¼ cups dry red wine

1 tbsp Worcestershire sauce

5 tbsp sunflower oil

4 red Scotch Bonnet chiles, seeded
and sliced

1 tbsp roughly chopped fresh oregano

8 oz rump steak, trimmed and cut into
thin strips

1 red onion, cut into thin wedges

1 small red bell pepper, seeded and
cut into thin strips

1 small yellow bell pepper, seeded and
cut into thin strips

1 zucchini, trimmed and cut
into thin strips

8 to 12 wheat tortillas, lightly warmed,
sour cream, Green Chili Sauce
(page 174) and Guacamole (page 18),
to serve

Mix the wine, Worcestershire sauce, 3 tbsp of the oil, half the chiles and the oregano in a bowl. Put the beef into a shallow dish and pour the wine marinade over. Cover and leave for at least 1 hour. Drain, reserving a little of the marinade.

Heat the remaining oil in a wok or large pan and quickly fry the remaining chiles and the vegetables for 3 to 5 minutes, or until crisp and slightly blackened on the edges. Remove from the pan and reserve.

Fry the beef in batches in the oil remaining in the pan for 2 to 3 minutes, or until sealed and browned. Drain on paper towels. When all the meat has been browned, return the vegetables and 3 to 4 tbsp of the reserved marinade to the pan and heat through over a fierce heat, stirring frequently.

To serve, spread each warmed tortilla with sour cream, then place some of the beef mixture on top and add a spoonful of the chili sauce. Roll up and eat with extra green chili sauce and guacamole.

KITCHEN SINK CHILI

Serves 12

This moderately spicy chili has beef, turkey sausage, tomatoes, mushrooms, olives, beans – everything but the kitchen sink.

INGREDIENTS

3 lb ground beef

1 lb turkey sausage

2 cups water

3 onions, chopped

6 garlic cloves, minced

½ green pepper, finely chopped

3 cups beef stock

8-oz can tomato sauce

14-oz can chopped tomatoes

¼ cup mild *chile molido*

1 tbsp hot chili powder

1 tbsp ground cumin

1 tbsp dried oregano

¼ tsp ground allspice

2 cups sliced mushrooms

2 x 2¼-oz cans sliced olives

3 x 16-oz cans kidney or pinto beans

salt, to taste

Crumble the beef and sausage into a large saucepan. Cook, stirring to break up any large lumps, until browned. Spoon off and discard the fat.

Add all the remaining ingredients, except the olives, beans, and salt. Stir well, bring to a boil, then reduce the heat and simmer for 1 hour, stirring occasionally and adding water if needed. Stir in the olives and beans, and simmer for 15 minutes more. Add some salt to taste, adjust the seasonings and serve.

SPICY LIVER SALAD

Serves 4

Liver loses its image as a less-than-exciting variety meat when it gets a flavor boost from chiles and fish sauce.

INGREDIENTS

¼ cup chicken stock

11 oz beef liver, thinly sliced

¼ cup sliced shallots

¼ cup freshly chopped mint leaves

3 scallions, finely chopped

¼ cup lime or lemon juice

2 tbsp sticky rice, dry-fried for a few minutes and pounded finely

2 tbsp crushed dried red chile

2 tbsp Thai fish sauce

lettuce leaves, for serving

Pour the chicken stock into a skillet and bring to a boil. Add the liver and cook until medium-rare. If you prefer to cook the liver for slightly longer, do so, but do not overcook or the meat will be tough and leathery.

Remove the pan from the heat and drain off all the liquid. Stir in the shallots, chopped mint, scallions and lime or lemon juice, with the pounded rice, crushed dried chile and fish sauce. Mix well.

Serve on a bed of lettuce and garnish with the sprig of mint.

COOK'S TIP

Beef liver has quite a strong flavor and is not to everyone's taste, but it is perfect for this spicy dish. You could also use chicken livers for a warm salad on mixed leaves; reduce the amount of crushed chile if you do, or use hot pepper sauce instead (see page 177).

BREDIE

Serves 6

Bredie is a South African stew made from mutton, tomato juice, and dried spotted beans similar to pinto beans. Its exotic combination of seasonings – cardamom, fennel, and ginger – often includes some form of chiles. This version, made with lamb shanks, is mildly spicy, but can be made hotter with hot pepper sauce.

INGREDIENTS

2 lamb shanks

2 bay leaves

1 cup dry pinto beans, picked over and soaked overnight

2 tbsp vegetable oil

1 large onion, chopped

2 garlic cloves, minced

1 tsp fresh gingerroot, grated

1 tsp ground coriander

¼ tsp ground cardamom

1 tsp fennel seed

½ tsp dried thyme

1 tsp dried oregano

2 tbsp chili powder

2 cups tomato juice

6-oz can tomato paste

1 to 2 tsp salt

hot pepper sauce to taste

Put the lamb shanks and bay leaves in a large saucepan and add water to cover. Bring to a boil, reduce the heat and simmer gently for 45 minutes.

Drain the beans and add them to the lamb, then pour in enough water to cover the mixture by 1 inch. Return to a boil, reduce the heat and simmer for 30 minutes. Remove the lamb shanks and let cool slightly while you prepare the other ingredients.

Heat the oil in a large skillet and sauté the onion and garlic for 2 minutes. Add the ginger, coriander, cardamom, fennel seed, thyme, and oregano. Sauté for 5 minutes more. Add to the beans, with the chili powder, tomato juice, and tomato paste. Return to a boil, reduce the heat and continue simmering, stirring occasionally and adding a little water if needed.

When the lamb has cooled enough to handle, cut the meat from the bones. Discard the fat, then shred the meat and add it to the bean mixture. Cook for 1 to 1¼ hours more, or until the beans are tender. Just before serving, stir in salt and hot pepper sauce to taste.

LAMB IN SPICY YOGURT SAUCE

Serves 4

INGREDIENTS

2 tbsp sunflower or olive oil

4 lean boneless lamb steaks, about
5 oz each

1 onion, sliced

2 garlic cloves, crushed

3 green New Mexico chiles, peeled,
seeded and sliced

1 tsp ground cumin

½ tsp ground cloves

1 tsp ground cinnamon

12 green cardamom pods

1 cup water

1¼ cups plain yogurt

2 tbsp ground almonds

2 tbsp flaked almonds, toasted

flat-leafed parsley, for the garnish

Heat the oil in a skillet and seal the lamb steaks on both sides. Lift out and drain on paper towels, then set aside.

Add the onion, garlic, and chiles to the oil remaining in the pan and sauté for 5 minutes, or until soft. Stir in the spices and cook for 3 minutes more. Stir in the water and bring to a boil. Reduce the heat and add the lamb, then simmer for 10 minutes.

Stir the yogurt and ground almonds into the pan and cook over low heat for a further 15 minutes, or until the lamb is tender. Stir frequently during this time. If the sauce is thickening too much, add a little extra water.

Transfer the mixture to a heated serving dish, sprinkle with the toasted almonds and garnish with parsley.

KASHMIRI LAMB

Serves 4

Kashmir dishes are usually rich and creamy and often include the cashews that grow so well in this area. They owe their red color to *ratan jot*, a red herb food coloring.

INGREDIENTS

3 tbsp sunflower oil or ghee

1 large onion, sliced

2 garlic cloves

2 or 3 red New Mexico chiles, seeded and sliced

1-inch piece fresh gingerroot, peeled and grated

1 tsp ground cumin

1 tsp turmeric

1 tsp *ratan jot* or few drops of red food coloring

1 lb lamb tenderloin, trimmed and cubed

4 tomatoes, peeled, seeded and chopped

2 cups lamb or vegetable stock

2 tbsp pistachio nuts

⅓ cup cashew nuts

2 tbsp golden raisins

1 tbsp freshly chopped cilantro

freshly cooked rice, to serve

Heat the oil or ghee in a large pan, and sauté the onion, garlic, chiles, and ginger for 5 minutes. Add the spices and sauté for 3 minutes more, then stir in the *ratan jot* or food-coloring. Add the lamb in two batches and cook for 5 minutes, or until sealed, stirring frequently. Add the tomatoes and stock, then bring to a boil. Cover, reduce the heat and simmer for 40 minutes.

Stir in the nuts and golden raisins. Simmer for 15 minutes more, or until the meat is tender. Stir in the cilantro and serve with freshly cooked rice.

NEW MEXICO CHILI WITH LAMB

Serves 4 to 6

Lamb is a staple of the Navajo Indians of New Mexico and is frequently prepared in stews. Fresh New Mexico green chiles are traditional, but Anaheim or poblano chiles or a combination can be substituted.

INGREDIENTS

2 tbsp vegetable oil

2 lb lamb, cubed

1½ medium onions, chopped

4 garlic cloves, minced

8 fresh New Mexico, Anaheim, or poblano chiles or a combination

8-oz can tomato sauce

2 to 4 fresh jalapeño or serrano chiles, minced

1 tsp dried oregano

¼ tsp dried sage

½ cup freshly chopped cilantro

about 1 tsp salt

Heat the oil in a large, deep skillet and cook the lamb until browned on all sides. If the skillet is large enough, add the onion and garlic and cook for 5 minutes more, then transfer to a large saucepan. If the skillet is not large enough, first remove the lamb to a large pan, then add additional oil to the skillet, if needed and sauté the onion and garlic before adding the mixture to the lamb. Pour in the water. Bring the liquid to a boil, reduce the heat and simmer for at least 1½ hours.

While the lamb is simmering, roast the green chiles (but not the jalapeños or serranos). Place them under a broiler and cook, turning, until all sides are blistered and blackened. Remove the chiles and immediately put them in a plastic bag or bowl (covered with paper towels) to steam for at least 10 minutes. Peel the chiles and remove the stems and seeds.

Chop half the roasted chiles and add them to the stew. Put the rest in a blender or food processor with the tomato sauce and purée until smooth. Add the purée to the stew, along with the jalapeños or serranos, the oregano, and sage. Approximately 10 minutes before the chili is cooked, add the fresh cilantro and salt. Taste and adjust the seasonings.

STEWED LAMB WITH HABANEROS

Serves 4 to 6

Beer is the secret ingredient in this spicy dish from the Netherlands Antilles. Use hot pepper sauce instead of minced chiles if you prefer.

INGREDIENTS

2 tbsp vegetable oil

2 lb boneless lamb,
cut into 2-inch cubes

2 medium onions, chopped

4 garlic cloves, chopped

½ cup chopped celery

1 tsp finely chopped fresh gingerroot

3 tbsp minced habanero chiles

1 small green bell pepper,
seeded and chopped

2 medium tomatoes, peeled and
chopped

1 tbsp lime or lemon juice

1 tsp ground cumin

1 tsp ground allspice

½ to ¾ cup beer

1 tbsp red wine vinegar

1 large cucumber, peeled and chopped

¼ cup pitted green olives (optional)

1 tbsp capers (optional)

Heat the vegetable oil in a Dutch oven over medium-high heat. Brown the lamb on all sides, then lift out the cubes with a slotted spoon and place them in a bowl. Add the onions, garlic, celery, ginger, chiles, and green bell pepper to the oil remaining in the pan, and sauté until the onions are soft.

Return the lamb cubes to the pan and stir in the tomatoes, lime or lemon juice, cumin, and allspice. Cover with beer. Bring to just below a boil, then reduce the heat and simmer for about 1½ hours, until the meat is very tender and starts to fall apart. Add more beer if necessary.

Stir in the vinegar and chopped cucumber, with the olives and capers if using. Simmer for 15 minutes more before serving.

PORK CHILI WITH SMOKED PAPRIKA

Serves 4

This chili is only mildly spicy, but the pungent flavor is rounded out by the addition of smoked paprika. Use regular paprika if you cannot locate smoked, but increase the quantity to 1 tablespoon.

INGREDIENTS

1 tbsp vegetable oil

2 lb pork, cubed

1½ onions, chopped

1 celery stalk, finely chopped

3 cups chicken stock

8-oz can tomato sauce

2 tsp smoked paprika

1 tbsp chili powder

1 tsp dried oregano

about 1 tsp salt

sour cream, for the topping

Heat the oil in a large, deep skillet or saucepan and cook the pork until lightly browned on all sides. Add the onion and celery and cook for 5 minutes, stirring frequently.

Add the stock, tomato sauce, smoked paprika and oregano. Bring to a boil, reduce the heat and simmer for 1½ to 2 hours, adding water if needed. Add salt to taste. Serve with a generous swirl of sour cream on each portion.

SZECHUAN HOT CHILI PORK

Serves 4

Szechuan cuisine is becoming increasingly popular in the West and there are many different variations on any Szechuan dish. Some err on the sweet side, but nearly all have a strong chili flavor.

INGREDIENTS

2 tbsp sunflower or groundnut oil

1-inch piece fresh gingerroot, peeled and grated

2 or 3 hontaka or Thai red chiles, seeded and chopped

12 oz pork tenderloin, trimmed and cut into thin strips

1 red bell pepper, seeded and cut into strips

1 yellow bell pepper, seeded and cut into strips

6 scallions, sliced diagonally

1 tbsp tomato paste mixed with 1 tbsp water

2 tsp soy sauce

1 tsp honey

1 tsp sesame oil

scallion tassel and flat-leafed parsley to garnish

Heat the oil in a wok or large pan and stir-fry the ginger and chiles for 2 minutes. Add the pork and stir-fry for a further 4 to 5 minutes. Then add the peppers and cook for 2 minutes. Add the scallions and stir-fry for 30 seconds. Then add the tomato paste mixture, the soy sauce, and honey. Stir-fry for 1 minute, than add the sesame oil and give one more stir. Serve immediately, garnished with a scallion tassel and flat-leafed parsley.

COOK'S TIP

A scallion tassel makes a very effective garnish: simply trim the scallion to a length of about 6 inches, then make a series of parallel lengthwise slits in the white part. Place the scallion in ice water for about 4 hours and the white strips will curl.

◀*Pork Chili with Smoked Paprika*

QUICK JERK PORK CHOPS

Serves 4

In the Caribbean, chiles are called hot peppers, and are often used to make a spice rub for flavoring chicken breasts, ribs or lamb or pork chops. Marinate the chops overnight if you have time. Next day, all you have to do is throw them on the grill or under the broiler.

INGREDIENTS

¼ cup chopped red chiles

⅓ cup fresh allspice berries or
3 tbsp ground allspice

3 tbsp lime juice

2 tbsp chopped green onion

I tsp Hot, Hot, Hot Pepper Sauce
(page 177)

I tsp ground cinnamon

I tsp ground nutmeg

4 center-cut pork chops

cucumber slices and small tomato
wedges, for the garnish

In a food processor or blender, purée the chiles, allspice, lime juice, green onion, hot pepper sauce, cinnamon, and nutmeg to make a thick paste. Rub the mixture into the chops and arrange them in a single layer in a shallow dish. Cover and marinate in the refrigerator for I hour or more.

Grill the chops over a hot charcoal fire or broil under a hot broiler until done. The seasonings will cause the chops to char on the outside.

SZECHUAN NOODLES WITH PORK AND CHILES

Serves 4

Chili-spiced pork served on a crisp cake of fried noodles is the perfect way to warm up on a cold winter's night.

INGREDIENTS

12 oz Chinese egg noodles

1 tbsp cornstarch

3 tbsp dry sherry

⅓ cup chicken stock

⅓ cup light soy sauce

⅓ cup oil

2 fresh green chiles, seeded and chopped

2 garlic cloves, crushed

2-inch piece fresh gingerroot, peeled and cut into fine strips

8 oz lean boneless pork, cut into fine strips

1 red bell pepper, seeded and cut into fine, short strips

1 bunch green onions, cut diagonally into fine slices

7-oz can bamboo shoots, drained and cut in strips

1-inch slice Chinese cabbage head, separated into pieces

Place the noodles in a pan and pour in enough boiling water to cover them. Bring back to a boil and cook for 2 minutes. While the noodles are cooking, mix the cornstarch with the sherry, stock and soy sauce, then set aside. Drain the noodles.

Wipe the pan and heat the oil. Add the noodles, spreading them out thinly, and fry over medium to high heat until they are crisp and golden underneath, patting them down slightly into a thin cake – they will set more or less in shape. Use a large slice to turn the noodle cake over and brown the second side. Don't worry if the noodles break up slightly – the aim is to end up with some that are crisp and others that remain soft. Transfer the noodles to a large serving dish and keep hot.

Add the chiles, garlic, ginger, and pork strips to the oil remaining in the pan. Stir-fry the mixture over high heat until the pork is browned. Add the red pepper and green onions and stir-fry for 2 minutes more, then the bamboo shoots. Stir-fry for 1 minute to heat the bamboo shoots.

Give the cornstarch mixture a stir and pour it into the pan. Bring to a boil, stirring, and cook over high heat for 30 seconds. Mix in the Chinese cabbage and stir for just long enough to heat it. Spoon the pork mixture over the noodles and serve at once.

FEIJOADA

Serves 8 to 10

Feijoada, a spicy stew of black beans and pork, is the ceremonial dish of Brazil. Traditionally it is made with various parts of the pig, such as snout, ears, tail, and feet. This hot Americanized version uses pork loin and linguica, a garlicky Portuguese sausage. Serve Feijoada with rice, greens, and orange slices. If you cannot find *chiles de arbol,* any small hot dried red chiles will do.

INGREDIENTS

2 cups dry black beans, picked over and soaked overnight

4 tbsp vegetable oil

3 whole dried *chiles de arbol*

8 garlic cloves, minced

2 lb pork loin, cubed

I large onion, chopped

14-ounce can chopped tomatoes

I lb linguica, cut into ¼-inch slices

3 jalapeño chiles, minced

about 2 tsp salt

orange twists, for the garnish

boiled rice, for serving

Drain the beans, put them in a heavy saucepan and add enough water to cover by 2 inches. Bring to a boil, reduce the heat and simmer.

Heat I tablespoon of the oil in a small skillet and sauté the *chiles de arbol* and half the minced garlic for I to 2 minutes, until the garlic just starts to brown. Add to the beans.

Heat another I tablespoon oil in a large skillet and cook the pork until lightly browned. Lift out the pork with a slotted spoon and add it to the black beans.

Heat the remaining oil in a skillet and sauté the onion with the remaining garlic for 5 minutes, then add to the beans.

Add the tomatoes and linguica to the beans. Return the stew to a boil, reduce the heat and simmer for I hour. Stir in the jalapeños and continue to simmer the stew for 30 minutes to I hour, until the beans are tender. Add the salt, taste the stew, and adjust the seasonings. Garnish with orange twists and serve with rice.

PORK AND CHILI BALLS

Serves 4

INGREDIENTS

1 lb lean ground pork

3 lemongrass stalks, outer leaves discarded, minced

1 tsp Red Chili Paste (page 174)

grated peel of 1 lime

3 tomatoes, peeled, seeded and finely chopped

1 tsp turmeric

2 tsp minced, fresh gingerroot

1 garlic clove, minced

¼ tsp salt

oil for deep-frying

lime wedges, whole star anise, cilantro sprigs, and chile flowers, for the garnish

boiled rice, for serving

Put the pork, lemongrass, chili paste and lime peel into a bowl. Stir in the tomatoes, turmeric, ginger, garlic, and salt. Mix well.

Using slightly wet hands, form the pork mixture into small balls, each about the size of an apricot. Place on a tray, cover and chill for 30 minutes.

Heat the oil for deep-frying to 350°F. Fry the pork balls in batches for 5 to 6 minutes, or until golden. Remove with a slotted spoon and drain on paper towels. Serve hot on a bed of rice, garnished with lime wedges, whole star anise, cilantro sprigs, and chile flowers.

BRAISED HAM WITH CHILI SAUCE

Serves 4

INGREDIENTS

3 fresh red poblano chiles

1 garlic clove

4 tbsp olive or sunflower oil

2 tbsp orange juice

2 tsp honey, warmed

4 ham steaks, trimmed of excess fat

2 tbsp butter

⅔ cup dry white wine

⅔ cup chicken or vegetable stock

3-inch piece of cucumber, thinly peeled and cut into julienne strips

1 tbsp cornstarch mixed with 1 tbsp water

orange wedges and fresh herbs, for the garnish

Preheat the broiler. Place the chiles in the broiler pan and broil for 10 minutes, or until the skins have blistered and charred. Put into a plastic bag for 10 minutes to soften, then peel and remove the seeds.

Chop the chiles roughly and put them in a food processor. Add the garlic, oil, orange juice, and honey. Process until smooth, then brush the marinade over both sides of the ham steaks. Leave in a cool place for at least 30 minutes.

Melt the butter in a large skillet and seal the steaks quickly on both sides. Add any remaining chili marinade and pour in the wine and stock. Bring to a boil, then reduce the heat and simmer for 5 to 8 minutes, or until the steaks are cooked. Drain and place on warmed serving plates.

Add the cucumber to the pan and stir in the cornstarch mixture. Cook, stirring occasionally, for 2 minutes, or until the sauce has thickened. Pour over the steaks and garnish with the orange wedges and fresh herbs.

VEGETARIAN CHOICE

SPICY VEGETABLE CRUNCH

Serves 4

INGREDIENTS

3 tbsp oil

3 to 4 whole dried chiles

1 tsp cumin seeds

¼ tsp turmeric

½ tsp salt

1 cup cauliflower flowerets

⅔ cup cut green beans

½ red bell pepper, seeded and diced

½ green bell pepper, seeded and diced

⅔ cup diced carrots

2 tomatoes, chopped

2 tsp grated fresh gingerroot

3 to 4 plump garlic cloves, minced

1 fresh green chile, chopped

2 to 3 tbsp freshly chopped cilantro

Heat the oil in a large heavy skillet. Break the whole dried chiles into the skillet and add the cumin seeds. When both begin to sizzle, add the turmeric and salt. Stir, then add all the vegetables, including the tomato. Stir-fry for 2 minutes.

Add the ginger, garlic, and green chiles and stir to mix thoroughly.

Lower the heat, cover the pan tightly and steam cook the vegetables for 12 to 15 minutes until crisp-tender. Sprinkle with the cilantro and serve.

BLACK-EYED PEAS IN GINGER SAUCE

Serves 4

Vegetarian dishes can be accused of being a bit bland. Not this one – the combination of gingerroot and chile gives black-eyed peas a marvelous flavor.

INGREDIENTS

1 cup dried black-eyed peas, picked over and soaked overnight

3½ cups water

2 tsp grated fresh gingerroot

½ tsp chili powder

¼ tsp turmeric

½ tsp salt

1 to 2 fresh green chiles, seeded

1 tbsp plain yogurt

1 tbsp oil

1 large onion, sliced

½ tsp cumin seeds

4 to 5 garlic cloves, chopped

¼ tsp garam masala

2 to 3 tbsp freshly chopped cilantro

Drain the black-eyed peas and place them in a heavy pan. Add the water and bring to a boil. Stir in half the ginger, the chili powder, turmeric, and salt, then reduce the heat, cover the pan and cook slowly for 45 to 50 minutes.

Add the remaining ginger, the green chiles, and the yogurt. Mix well and let the mixture simmer for another 10 to 15 minutes, or until the beans are tender.

Heat the oil in a small skillet and sauté the onion for 3 to 4 minutes over medium heat. When it is starting to color, add the cumin seeds and chopped garlic. Remove the pan from the heat just as the garlic is turning golden brown.

Pour the mixture into the simmering peas, then stir in the garam masala. Cook for 5 minutes, then stir in the cilantro and serve.

COOK'S TIP
Use tamarind pulp instead of yogurt if you can locate any. If you use the instant concentrated tamarind, you will only need to add 1 tsp.

CAULIFLOWER AND TOMATO CURRY

Serves 4

If dried chiles are not available, use 3 or 4 green fresno chiles or 1 to 1½ tsp medium-hot chili powder.

INGREDIENTS

5 dried ancho chiles

3 cups cauliflower flowerets

1½ cups diced potatoes

2 tbsp sunflower oil

2-inch piece of gingerroot, peeled and sliced

1 onion, sliced

2 garlic cloves, minced

1 tsp coriander seeds

1 tsp cumin seeds

1 tsp fenugreek seeds

1 tsp turmeric

2 tbsp tomato paste mixed with 2 tbsp water

3 cups peeled, seeded and chopped tomatoes

⅔ cup coconut milk

⅔ cup plain yogurt, plus extra for the garnish

fresh flat-leafed parsley or cilantro, to garnish

poppadoms, for serving

Roast the dried chiles in a nonstick skillet for 2 to 3 minutes, taking care not to let them scorch. Tip into a bowl and add hot (not boiling) water. Soak for at least 10 minutes until soft, then chop the chiles and set them aside.

Bring a saucepan of lightly salted water to a boil. Add the cauliflower flowerets and cook for 3 minutes, then lift out with a slotted spoon. Add the potatoes to the pan and boil for 10 minutes. Drain and reserve.

Heat the oil in the cleaned pan and gently sauté the ginger for 3 minutes, then lift out and discard the ginger. Add the onion, garlic, and chopped rehydrated chiles to the flavored oil, and sauté for 3 minutes. Stir in the spices and cook, stirring frequently, for 3 minutes.

Add the tomato paste mixture to the pan with the tomatoes and coconut milk. Bring to just below boiling point and cook for 5 minutes. Add the reserved cauliflower and potatoes, and cook for 5 to 8 minutes longer, or until the vegetables are just tender.

Stir in the yogurt and heat through gently for 2 minutes. Drizzle the extra yogurt over when serving and garnish with fresh parsley or cilantro. Serve with poppadoms.

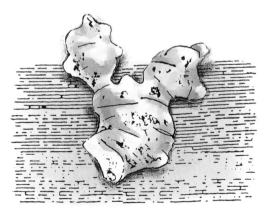

CHEESE-FILLED CHILES IN BATTER JACKETS

Serves 4

You need large chiles for this Mexican recipe: Anaheims or poblanos are best. Stuffing them takes time, but the taste is sensational and well worth the effort. Canned chiles won't give quite such good results, but are worth using if you are in a hurry.

INGREDIENTS

12 fresh Anaheim or poblano chiles

4 cups finely grated Cheddar or Monterey Jack cheese

1 cup all-purpose flour

6 eggs, separated

oil for deep-frying

boiled rice and refried beans, for serving

Preheat the broiler. Place the chiles in the broiler pan and broil until the skins blister and start to blacken. Place in a strong plastic bag – or in a bowl, covered with paper towels – and leave for 10 minutes.

Slit the side of each chile carefully and remove the seeds and veins, taking care not to break the flesh. Shape a small amount of grated cheese to fit the chile, tapering it as needed, and ease into place. Stuff the remaining chiles in the same way.

Spread out the flour in a shallow bowl. Beat the egg yolks in a second bowl until pale and thick. In a bowl, whisk the egg whites until stiff, then fold them into the yolks to make a simple batter. Heat the oil for deep-frying. Working quickly, roll each filled chile in flour, then dip it in the batter, making sure that the entire surface is coated. Deep-fry the coated chiles in batches, until the batter coating is crisp and golden, then drain on paper towels. Keep hot while cooking successive batches. Serve immediately, with rice and refried beans.

CHILI WITH PEACHES AND THREE BEANS

Serves 12

This vegetarian chili is so delicious, everyone will want some. Serve it on its own, with rice or noodles, or as a filling for baked potatoes.

INGREDIENTS

1 red bell pepper, roughly chopped

2 green bell peppers, roughly chopped

1 large onion, roughly chopped

2 peaches, peeled and roughly chopped

28-oz can tomatoes, coarsely chopped

28-oz can tomato sauce

1 tsp hot pepper sauce

¼ tsp dried thyme

1 tsp dried oregano

2 tsp ground cumin, or more to taste

1 tbsp chili powder

1 tsp ground black pepper

1 cup water

19-oz can cannellini beans

2 x 16-oz cans black beans

16-oz can kidney beans

salt (optional)

Put all the ingredients, except the beans, in a heavy saucepan and stir well. Bring to a boil, reduce the heat and simmer for 30 minutes, stirring often to keep the chili from scorching, and adding more water if needed.

Add the beans, with enough can liquid for the desired consistency. Simmer for 15 minutes more. Taste and add salt, if needed.

OKRA AND BEAN CURRY

Serves 4

It is possible to make a delicious vegetable curry in under half an hour, as this simple recipe proves.

INGREDIENTS

2 tbsp sunflower oil

1 large onion, sliced

2 garlic cloves, crushed

4 fresh Kenyan or green fresno chiles, seeded and sliced

1 tsp ground coriander

1 tsp ground cumin

5 cloves, ground

8 green cardamom pods

1 tsp turmeric

1 tsp fenugreek seeds, lightly bruised

2 cups vegetable stock

1 lb okra, trimmed

⅔ cup drained canned pinto or kidney beans, rinsed

4 tbsp plain yogurt

2 tbsp freshly chopped cilantro

2 tbsp flaked almonds, toasted

Heat the oil in a pan and sauté the onion, garlic and chiles for 5 minutes. Add the spices and sauté for 3 minutes more. Stir in the stock and bring to a boil. Cover the pan, reduce the heat and simmer for 10 minutes more.

Prick the okra a few times with a fork and add to the pan with the beans. Cook gently for 8 to 10 minutes, or until the okra is tender.

Stir in the yogurt and cilantro, and heat through briefly, without boiling. Serve sprinkled with the almonds.

SPINACH AND POTATO SAMOSAS

Serves 4

Folding filo pastry to make samosas is fun and doesn't take long to master the technique.
Try these with Caribbean Mango Chutney (page 185).

INGREDIENTS

3 tbsp sunflower oil

1 onion, chopped

3 fresh green fresno chiles, seeded and chopped

1 tsp ground cumin

1 tsp ground coriander

¾ cup diced potatoes, cooked and well drained

2 cups chopped spinach, cooked and well drained

4 large sheets filo pastry, thawed if frozen

oil for deep-frying

Heat the oil in a deep skillet and sauté the onion and chiles for 3 minutes, then stir in the spices and cook for 3 minutes more. Stir in the cooked vegetables and mix well. Let cool. Cut the filo into 10- x 4-inch strips. Place 2 tbsp of the vegetable filling at one end of each strip and fold the dough over diagonally to enclose the filling and form a triangle. Fold the triangle over on itself. Continue along the strip until you have a neat triangular pastry, sealing the final turn with a little water. Heat the oil for deep-frying to 350°F and fry the samosas in batches for about 5 minutes, until golden. Drain on paper towels and serve with chutney or salsa. A mixed leaf salad would be the ideal accompaniment.

LENTIL AND VEGETABLE CHILI

Serves 4 to 6

A combination of kidney beans, lentils, peas, and carrots makes a chunky vegetarian chili that can be as mild or as fiery as you choose.

INGREDIENTS

1 cup dry kidney beans, picked over and soaked overnight

1 bay leaf

1 tbsp vegetable oil

1 celery stalk, chopped

1 onion, chopped

1 garlic clove, minced

2 tsp chili powder

½ tsp dried oregano

½ tsp dried basil

14-oz can chopped tomatoes

⅓ cup red lentils

¾ cup sliced carrots

¾ cup shelled peas, thawed if frozen

salt

cooked peas and carrots, for serving

Drain the beans, put them in a large saucepan and pour in water to cover. Add the bay leaf. Bring to a boil and boil hard for 10 minutes, then reduce the heat and simmer while you prepare the remaining ingredients.

Heat the oil in a skillet and sauté the celery and onion for 5 minutes.

Add the garlic and sauté for 5 minutes. Add the contents of the skillet to the beans, with the chili powder, oregano, basil, and tomatoes. Return to a boil, reduce the heat and simmer for 1 hour, adding water if the mixture becomes too thick.

Stir in the lentils and cook for 10 minutes. Add water if necessary, then add the carrots and cook for 5 minutes more. Stir in the peas and cook for 10 minutes by which time the lentils should have cooked down to a purée and the beans should be tender. Add salt to taste. Serve with peas and carrots.

SPICED VEGETABLES WITH BEAN CURD

Serves 6

Bean curd has little taste of its own, but readily absorbs the flavor of the spicy sauce to make a valuable contribution to this vegetarian dish. Use smoked bean curd if you prefer.

INGREDIENTS

6 dried ancho, pasilla, or New Mexico chiles, or a combination

1 cup hot water

about 4 tbsp vegetable oil

1 large onion, chopped

1 green bell pepper, seeded and chopped

2 celery stalks, chopped

4 garlic cloves, minced

2 cups vegetable stock

1 cup tomato sauce

14-oz can chopped tomatoes

1 tsp ground cumin

1 tsp ground coriander

1 tsp paprika

2 tsp dried oregano

12 oz firm tofu

1 tsp salt

¼ cup freshly chopped cilantro

Split the dried chiles in half and remove the stems and seeds. Put the pieces in a small bowl and pour over the hot but not boiling water. Let them steep in the water for 30 minutes, stirring occasionally to be sure all parts of the chiles remain covered with water.

Meanwhile, heat 2 tablespoons of the oil in a large skillet. Sauté the onion, bell pepper, celery, and garlic for 5 minutes. Put the sautéed vegetables in a large pan and add the stock, tomato sauce, tomatoes, spices and oregano. Stir in the salt. Bring to a boil, reduce the heat and simmer while you make the chili sauce.

Pour the chiles, with their soaking liquid, into a blender or food processor. Purée until a smooth sauce is formed. Strain the sauce and add it to the simmering vegetable mixture.

Cut the tofu into ¼-inch cubes. Heat the remaining oil in a skillet and fry the tofu over medium to high heat for 2 to 3 minutes each side until the cubes are slightly browned. Add the tofu to the chili and simmer for 30 minutes more. Stir in the cilantro and salt to taste. Adjust the seasonings if necessary and serve.

COOK'S TIP

If not using firm bean curd, it should be pressed to remove excess water. Place the tofu on a plate, put another plate on top and weight it with cans or other heavy objects. Tofu should be pressed for at least 30 minutes before frying.

SEASONAL VEGETABLES IN GREEN MASALA

Serves 4

This is a very good tempered recipe; you can vary the vegetables as long as you keep the proportions the same.

INGREDIENTS

2 tbsp oil

3 or 4 whole dried chiles

1 tsp cumin seeds

2 cups cauliflower flowerets

⅔ cup cut green beans

¾ cup diced carrots

½ red bell pepper, seeded and diced

½ green bell pepper, seeded and diced

1 beefsteak tomato, chopped

¼ tsp turmeric

½ to ¾ tsp salt

GREEN MASALA

2 tsp grated fresh gingerroot

4 fat garlic cloves, chopped

2 fresh green chiles, chopped

3 tbsp freshly chopped cilantro

Heat the oil in a heavy saucepan. Crumble the whole dried chiles into the pan and add the cumin seeds. Fry for 1 minute, then add all the vegetables, with the turmeric, and salt. Cook for 1 to 2 minutes more, while stirring the vegetables together.

Add all the ingredients for the green masala. Stir continuously until the ingredients are well mixed. Cover the pan and simmer over a medium heat for 15 minutes, until the vegetables are crisp-tender. Serve immediately while hot.

POTATO CURRY

Serves 4

What could be simpler or more satisfying than this tasty curry ?

INGREDIENTS

1 tsp cumin seeds

1 tsp whole coriander seeds

1 tsp fenugreek seeds

5 cloves

6 cardamom pods

2 tbsp sunflower oil

1 large onion, sliced

2 garlic cloves, crushed

4 fresh red jalapeño chiles, seeded and chopped

4½ cups cubed potatoes

2½ cups vegetable stock

1 red bell pepper, seeded and sliced

2 tbsp freshly chopped cilantro

Grind the whole spices in a spice mill or use a mortar and pestle. Heat the oil in a large pan and sauté the onion, garlic, and chiles for 5 minutes, or until softened. Add the ground spices and cook gently for 3 minutes more, stirring occasionally.

Add the potatoes with the stock and bring to a boil. Cover the pan, reduce the heat and simmer for 15 minutes, or until the potatoes are just tender.

Add the sliced red bell pepper and cook for 5 minutes more. Stir in the freshly chopped cilantro and serve.

◀ *Seasonal Vegetables in Green Masala*

MIXED MASALA BEANS

Serves 4 to 6

Not only do the ingredients blend so well together, they also make a very colorful dish.

INGREDIENTS

1 tbsp oil

½ onion, chopped

½ tsp cumin seeds

½ tsp chili powder

¼ tsp turmeric

¼ tsp garam masala

1¼ cups water

15-oz can chick-peas, drained

15-oz can kidney beans, drained

1 tomato, chopped

1 or 2 fresh green chiles, chopped

4 garlic cloves

1 tsp grated fresh gingerroot

1 green bell pepper, seeded and chopped

2 tsp lemon juice

2 to 3 tbsp freshly chopped cilantro

Heat the oil in a heavy saucepan. Stir in the onion with the cumin seeds and sauté until the onions are pale gold in color.

Stir in the chili powder, turmeric, and garam masala. Add 2 tbsp of the water and cook, stirring continuously for 1 to 2 minutes.

Gently stir in the chick-peas, kidney beans, tomato, green chiles, garlic, and ginger. Mix well and stir in the remaining water. Bring to a boil, then reduce the heat and simmer for 15 to 20 minutes.

Add the green bell pepper and cook for 2 to 3 minutes more. Stir in the lemon juice and half the cilantro. Tip into a heated serving dish, sprinkle with the remaining cilantro and serve.

PASTA WITH SPICY TOMATO SAUCE

Serves 4

INGREDIENTS

2 tbsp olive oil

1 large onion, chopped

1 small fennel bulb, trimmed and chopped

2 garlic cloves, crushed

4 red de agua chiles, seeded and sliced

8 sun-dried tomatoes

2 to 2¼ cups vegetable stock

1½ cups grated carrot

1½ cups wiped and sliced oyster mushrooms

2 tbsp tomato paste mixed with 4 tbsp water

1 tsp sugar

salt and pepper

2 red bell peppers, seeded, blanched and cut into small strips

2 tbsp freshly chopped basil

10 to 12 oz fresh pasta, such as tagliatelle or rigatoni

shaved or freshly grated Parmesan cheese, for serving

freshly chopped basil, for the garnish

Heat the oil in a pan and gently sauté the onion, fennel, garlic, chiles, and sun-dried tomatoes for 3 minutes. Add ⅔ cup of the stock and simmer for 5 to 8 minutes.

Put into a food processor and process to a chunky purée, adding extra stock if necessary. Return to the pan with the remaining stock.

Add the carrot, mushrooms, tomato paste mixture, sugar and seasoning to taste. Bring to a boil, then reduce the heat and simmer gently for 15 to 20 minutes, or until the sauce is thick. Add the bell peppers and chopped basil, and cook for 3 to 4 minutes more.

Meanwhile, cook the pasta in boiling salted water for 4 to 6 minutes, or until it rises to the surface of the water and is just tender. Drain and return to the cleaned pan.

Pour over the tomato sauce and toss well over the heat for 2 to 3 minutes. Garnish with freshly chopped basil and serve sprinkled with Parmesan cheese.

FRIED THAI NOODLES WITH CHILES

Serves 4

Lemongrass and ginger perfume this superb dish from Thailand.

INGREDIENTS

6 oz instant dried noodles

2 tbsp sunflower oil

2 lemongrass stalks, outer leaves removed, finely chopped

1-inch piece gingerroot, peeled and grated

1 red onion, cut into thin wedges

2 garlic cloves, crushed

4 red Thai chiles, seeded and sliced

1 red bell pepper, seeded and cut into matchsticks

1 small carrot, pared with a vegetable peeler into ribbons

1 small zucchini, pared with a vegetable peeler into ribbons

1 cup snow peas, trimmed and cut diagonally in half

6 scallions, trimmed and diagonally sliced

1 cup cashew nuts

2 tbsp soy sauce

juice of 1 orange

1 tsp honey

1 tbsp sesame oil

Cook the noodles in a saucepan of lightly salted boiling water for 3 minutes. Drain, plunge into cold water, then drain again and reserve.

Heat the oil in a wok or large pan and stir-fry the lemongrass and gingerroot for 2 minutes. Using a slotted spoon lift out and discard the lemongrass and gingerroot.

Add the onion, garlic, and chiles to the oil remaining in the wok or pan and stir-fry for 2 minutes. Add the red bell pepper and cook for 2 minutes more, than add the remaining vegetables and stir-fry for 2 minutes.

Add the reserved noodles with the cashew nuts, soy sauce, orange juice, and honey. Toss over the heat for 1 minute. Drizzle over the sesame oil and cook for 30 seconds. Serve immediately while hot.

SPICY BROWN RICE

Serves 4

INGREDIENTS

2 tbsp oil

2 cloves garlic, crushed

1 onion, finely chopped

½ small red bell pepper, seeded and thinly sliced

2 Anaheim chiles, seeded and chopped

1 cup brown rice

3 cups vegetable stock

salt and pepper

Heat the oil in a large skillet and sauté the garlic, onion, and red bell pepper and chiles for 5 to 7 minutes until the onion is transparent and beginning to brown.

Add the rice and cook for several minutes, stirring constantly.

Pour in the vegetable stock, cover the pan tightly and cook over a low heat for 30 to 35 minutes, until the rice is just tender. Season with salt and pepper and serve.

► *Fried Thai Noodles with Chiles*

CELLOPHANE NOODLES WITH VEGETABLES

Serves 4

Contrasting textures are a feature of this colorful noodle dish. After the vegetables have been prepared,
it takes very little time to cook.

INGREDIENTS

6 dried Chinese black mushrooms,
soaked in hot water for 30 minutes

5 oz young fresh spinach leaves

2 Chinese cabbage leaves

3 shiitake or oyster mushrooms, thinly
sliced

4 scallions, white and green parts
thickly sliced diagonally

1 small zucchini, cut into fine strips

1 carrot, cut into fine strips

4 tbsp vegetable oil

1 tbsp sesame oil

3 garlic cloves, minced

2 small fresh red chiles, seeded and
cut into fine strips

2 oz cellophane noodles, soaked in
hot water for 30 minutes and drained

1 tbsp soy sauce

1 tsp sugar

salt

Drain the dried mushrooms, and cut out and discard the stems and any hard parts. Thinly slice the mushroom caps.

Bring a large saucepan of water to a boil. Add the spinach, cover and quickly return to a boil. Boil for 2 minutes, then drain and rinse under cold running water and drain again, squeezing out as much water as possible. Separate the leaves and tear any large ones in half.

Cut away and discard the curly outer part of the Chinese cabbage leaves, saving only the "V" shaped core of the leaves. Cut this into fine strips, then place in a bowl with the spinach, dried and fresh mushrooms, scallions, zucchini, and carrot. Mix well.

Heat the vegetable oil and sesame oil in a deep skillet. Add the garlic and chiles and stir-fry for 10 seconds. Add the spinach mixture and stir-fry for 3 to 4 minutes until the vegetables are crisp-tender. Switch the heat to low and stir in the noodles, soy sauce, sugar, and salt. Toss over the heat for 2 minutes, then serve.

CHILI-RICE BURGERS

Serves 6

These burgers can be grilled on the barbecue, but it is a good idea to put them in a basket grill
so that they can be turned over easily.

INGREDIENTS

2 tbsp sunflower oil

2 garlic cloves, minced

4 red de agua chiles, seeded and chopped

heaping ¾ cup short-grain rice

1 large carrot, grated

2 tbsp tomato paste mixed with 2 tbsp water

2½ cups vegetable stock

salt and pepper

1 cup drained canned red kidney beans

½ cup whole-kernel corn

2 tbsp freshly chopped cilantro

2 tsp olive oil

1 large tomato, sliced

6 buns, lightly toasted

Chili Pepper Relish (page 32), for serving

Heat the sunflower oil in a skillet and sauté the garlic and chiles for 5 minutes. Stir in the rice and continue to cook for 3 minutes, stirring occasionally. Stir in the carrot.

Stir the tomato paste mixture into the pan with the stock. Add seasoning and bring to a boil. Reduce the heat and simmer for 20 minutes, or until the rice is cooked, stirring occasionally and adding a little extra stock if the rice is very dry.

Add the kidney beans and corn kernels. Cook for 5 minutes more or until the mixture is very stiff and will stick together. Stir in the chopped cilantro and remove from the heat. Let cool.

When the mixture is cool enough to handle, wet your hands slightly and shape into six large burgers. Cover and chill for at least 30 minutes.

Preheat the broiler to medium. Place the burgers under the broiler and brush lightly with a little olive oil. Broil for 4 to 5 minutes, or until heated through, carefully turning the burgers over once during cooking.

Place a slice of tomato on the bottom of each bun and top with a rice burger. Spoon a little relish over, cover with the bun tops and serve with extra relish.

HOT CHILE

CHEESE TURNOVERS WITH
GREEN TOMATO SAUCE

Serves 4

Use bought tortillas to make these turnovers, or prepare your own, following the directions on page 24.

INGREDIENTS

2 cups grated Cheddar cheese

6 scallions, trimmed and chopped

⅓ cup pine nuts, toasted

6 dried chipotle chiles, roasted and soaked in hot water for 10 minutes

2 tbsp butter

4 cups sliced mushrooms

8 prepared wheat tortillas

1 egg, beaten

oil for deep-frying

salad leaves, to serve

SAUCE

1½ cups peeled, seeded and chopped green tomatoes

3 shallots, finely chopped

2 or 3 garlic cloves, crushed

3 fresh green jalapeño chiles, seeded and chopped

⅔ cup vegetable stock

1 tsp honey

2 tsp arrowroot mixed with 1 tbsp water

2 tbsp freshly chopped flat-leafed parsley

Make the sauce. Put the green tomatoes, shallots, garlic, and chiles into a saucepan and simmer for 5 to 7 minutes, or until softened. Tip into a food processor and add the stock and honey. Process to a purée. Press through a fine strainer into the cleaned pan.

Return the sauce to the pan and simmer for 5 minutes. Stir in the arrowroot mixture and cook, stirring constantly until the sauce thickens and then clears.

Mix the cheese, scallions, and pine nuts in a bowl. Discard the seeds from the rehydrated chiles and chop the flesh. Add to the cheese mixture and mix well. Set aside.

Melt the butter in a small pan and sauté the mushrooms for 3 minutes. Drain. Place a spoonful of the cheese mixture on top of each tortilla and top with a spoonful of the mushrooms. Brush the edges of each tortilla with a little beaten egg, then fold over to form a crescent shape. Pinch the edges together firmly. Brush the edges lightly with the beaten egg and fold the edges over again to give a rope effect and a more secure seal.

Heat the oil to 350°F and fry the turnovers in batches for 2 to 3 minutes, or until golden. Drain on paper towels and serve on a bed of salad leaves. Hand around the green sauce separately.

HOT CHILE

MUSHROOM MASALA OMELET

Serves 2

Choose a skillet which can safely be placed under the broiler for making this omelet. The mixture is first fried, then finished under a hot broiler.

INGREDIENTS

3 eggs, separated

1 tsp all-purpose flour

¼ cup green or red bell pepper

½ cup chopped mushrooms

1 fresh green chile, finely chopped

½ cup thinly sliced onion

½ tsp chili powder

¼ tsp garlic powder

1 to 2 tbsp freshly chopped cilantro

¼ tsp cumin seeds

¼ tsp salt

2 tbsp water

1 tbsp oil

Whisk the egg yolks in a bowl, then fold in the flour and mix well. Add the chopped bell pepper, mushrooms, green chile, onion slices, and all the spices and herbs. Season with salt.

Whisk the egg whites in a grease-free bowl. Fold into the egg yolk mixture, and whisk once again, gradually adding the water.

Preheat the broiler. Grease a large, nonstick skillet with the oil and heat it to smoking point. Pour in the egg and vegetable mixture, reduce the heat and cook for 1 to 2 minutes, shaking the pan. Then slide the pan under the hot broiler to finish the omelet.

FRIED EGGS IN A SPICED VEGETABLE NEST

Serves 2

A simple dish which is often cooked for brunch in Indian households.

INGREDIENTS

1 tbsp butter

½ onion, thinly sliced

2 fresh green chiles, chopped

¼ cup red bell pepper matchsticks

2 garlic cloves

pinch of chili powder

pinch of salt

2 tbsp water

2 eggs

freshly ground black pepper

2 tbsp snipped chives

Melt the butter in a nonstick skillet and cook the onion and green chiles over low heat for 4 to 5 minutes, adding a tiny amount of water between stirs to keep them from sticking and burning.

Add the bell pepper and garlic and cook for 3 to 4 minutes, stirring continuously. Stir in the chili powder, salt and water and simmer again for 2 to 3 minutes.

Break the eggs gently on top of the bed of spiced vegetables in the pan, taking care to keep the egg yolks intact. Shake the pan so that the egg white spreads to fill the pan. Do not overcook the egg yolks – they are done when, if you were to pierce them with a fork, they would ooze out and run slightly.

Grind black pepper over the surface, sprinkle the chives over and serve immediately.

ZUCCHINI AND CHILE PANCAKES

Serves 4

These tasty little pancakes are ideal for serving with a vegetable stir-fry.

INGREDIENTS

4 cups shredded zucchini

1 or 2 fresh green chiles, seeded and sliced

1 tbsp minced garlic

2 scallions, finely chopped

salt and pepper

1 egg, lightly beaten

3 tbsp all-purpose flour

¼ cup vegetable oil

Put the shredded zucchini in a bowl and add the chiles, garlic, and chopped scallions. Season with plenty of salt and pepper. Add the beaten egg and stir in lightly. Stir in the flour.

Heat the oil in a deep, heavy skillet. Drop 1 tbsp of the mixture into the pan and flatten it lightly with the back of a spoon. Add more mixture to make as many pancakes as the skillet will hold comfortably.

Fry over medium heat for 2 to 3 minutes on each side, or until golden brown, turning over carefully so that the oil does not splatter. Drain on paper towels and keep hot. Before frying each new batch, stir the pancake mixture.

COOK'S TIP
The mixture can also be used to make larger pancakes. Spread them with sour cream, sprinkle grated Cheddar cheese over and roll up neatly before serving hot.

RANCH-STYLE EGGS

Serves 4

This started out as a breakfast dish in Mexico, but it is now served at any time, often with refried beans.

INGREDIENTS

4 tbsp corn oil

4 wheat or corn flour tortillas

3 shallots, finely chopped

I garlic clove, crushed

I or 2 red New Mexico chiles, seeded and chopped

1½ cups peeled, seeded and chopped ripe tomatoes

I tbsp tomato paste mixed with 2 tbsp water

salt and pepper

4 eggs

4 tbsp refried beans (page 26)

sprigs of parsley, for the garnish

Heat I tsp of the oil in a skillet and fry a tortilla for 30 seconds on both sides until crisp. Drain and keep warm. Fry the remaining tortillas in the same way.

Heat 2 tbsp of the remaining oil and sauté the shallots, garlic, and chiles for 5 minutes. Stir in the tomatoes and tomato paste mixture and leave to simmer while you cook the eggs.

Heat the remaining oil and fry the eggs until cooked to your taste. Place a tortilla on a plate, top with an egg and some tomato sauce. Serve with refried beans and garnish with parsley.

SALADS & VEGETABLES

GREEN MANGO SALAD

Serves 4

This salad is intentionally sour, but you can add more sugar if you like. The quantities do not need to be precise. Add the ingredients in the proportions that suit you, to create the flavor balance you and your family will enjoy.

INGREDIENTS

¼ cup unsweetened shredded coconut

2 cups green unripe mango flesh, cut into long matchsticks

¼ cup dried baby shrimp

3 tbsp sliced shallots

5 fresh small green chiles, chopped

1 tbsp palm or soft dark brown sugar, or to taste

fish sauce, to taste (optional)

lime juice, to taste (optional)

Dry-fry the shredded coconut in a skillet until it is pale brown in color. Watch it carefully so that it does not scorch.

Mix the coconut and mango matchsticks in a bowl. Add the dried shrimp, sliced shallots, and chopped chiles. Mix well and taste. If not salty enough add a little fish sauce; if not sour enough, add lime juice.

COOK'S TIP
If you cannot find unripe mangos, try this with peaches or nectarines.

BEAN SPROUT SALAD

Serves 4 to 6

This is one of Korea's best loved salads. Crunchy and nutritious, it is often served with pre-dinner drinks in restaurants, so guests have something to nibble while waiting for their meal to arrive.

INGREDIENTS

1½ lb soybean sprouts or mung bean sprouts

2 garlic cloves, minced

5 scallions, white and green parts thinly sliced into rings

1 fresh hot red chile, seeded and thinly sliced into rings

1 tbsp toasted sesame seeds

salt

Remove the roots from the bean sprouts, if necessary. Bring a saucepan of water to the boil, and add the bean sprouts. As soon as the water boils again, tip the bean sprouts into a colander and rinse under running cold water. Drain well, then squeeze out as much water as possible.

Tip the bean sprouts into a salad bowl and add the remaining ingredients. Serve at room temperature or slightly chilled. It is not necessary to add a dressing.

CORN SALAD WITH ROASTED CHILES AND PEPPERS

Serves 6

This corn salad is spicy but not too hot and can be used as a relish with grilled meats. When possible, use corn cut from the cob, but frozen corn is acceptable. The salad is best when made several hours in advance so the flavors have a chance to blend, but not so long that it loses its crunch. If the salad is made ahead, the avocado should be cut and added just before serving.

INGREDIENTS

1 poblano chile

1 sweet red bell pepper

3 cups fresh or frozen whole kernel corn

½ cup water

½ green bell pepper, seeded and diced

2 tomatoes, seeded and chopped

½ cup minced red onion

1 large avocado

DRESSING

¼ cup olive oil

3 tbsp lime juice

2 tbsp freshly chopped cilantro

½ tsp ground cumin

1 garlic clove, minced

dash salt

dash pepper

Make the dressing by mixing the olive oil, lime juice, cilantro, cumin, garlic, salt, and pepper in a jar. Close the lid tightly and shake well. Set aside.

Roast the chile and red bell pepper under the broiler for about 10 minutes, turning often, until all sides are charred. Remove and place in a plastic bag, or in a bowl covered with several paper towels. Let steam for at least 10 minutes.

While the chile and pepper are cooling, cook the corn. Put the water in a small pan, add the corn and bring to a boil. Cook for 5 minutes, then drain the corn and let it cool.

Remove the chile and red bell pepper from the bag or bowl. Rub off the blackened skin, then remove the stems and seeds. Cut the chile and pepper into narrow strips.

Place the chile and pepper strips in a bowl, add the corn, then the green bell pepper, tomatoes, and onion. Cut the avocado in half, remove the peel and seed, and dice the flesh. Add to the salad. Pour over the dressing and toss lightly. Serve as soon as possible after adding the diced avocado.

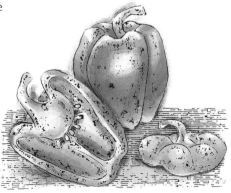

CUCUMBER SALAD WITH CHILES

Serves 4

It is important to observe the standing time when making this salad, so that all the flavors can blend.

INGREDIENTS

I large cucumber, peeled

I small red onion, thinly sliced

2 or 3 red serrano chiles, seeded and thinly sliced

2 tbsp lime juice

I tbsp Thai fish sauce

2 tsp honey, warmed

I tbsp sesame oil

arugula leaves

⅓ cup chopped roasted peanuts

Cut the cucumber in half lengthwise and cut into half-moon shapes. Place in a large shallow dish. Scatter the onion and chile slices over the top.

Mix the lime juice, fish sauce, and honey in a bowl. Whisk in the oil. Pour over the cucumber mixture, toss to coat, then leave in a cool place for at least 30 minutes to allow the flavors to develop.

Arrange the arugula leaves on a serving platter, top with the cucumber mixture and sprinkle with the roasted peanuts.

MIXED LEAVES WITH CHIPOTLE CHILE DRESSING

Serves 4

Chipotle chiles give a delicious smoky flavor to the dressing. You can substitute any other dried chile, if preferred, or use fresno chiles for a fresher flavor.

INGREDIENTS

4 oz arugula

a few small frisée and radicchio leaves

1 heart of lettuce

4 oz baby spinach leaves

2 heads Belgian endive

1 small red onion, thinly sliced

3 tbsp assorted freshly chopped fresh herbs, such as cilantro, flat-leafed parsley, oregano and marjoram

DRESSING

6 dried chipotle chiles

1 small onion, sliced

2 garlic cloves, minced

3 tbsp medium-dry white wine

3 tbsp white wine vinegar

2 tbsp tomato paste

⅔ cup water

Make the dressing. Split the chiles and discard the seeds. Put into a pan with the remaining dressing ingredients. Cover the pan and cook over gentle heat for 45 minutes, or until the chiles are soft and the liquid is reduced by half.

Tip the contents of the pan into a blender or food processor. Process to a smooth purée, then press through a strainer set over a bowl. Reserve.

Lightly rinse all the salad leaves and the endive. Pat dry with paper towels. Tear the leaves if large, then toss together in a salad bowl.

Divide the endive into single leaves and add to the salad with the onion and herbs. Mix together lightly. Just before serving, drizzle with the dressing and toss to coat.

GREEN BEAN SALAD WITH PICKLED JALAPEÑOS

Serves 4 to 6

This is a variation on a famous Mexican salad based on *nopalitos,* which are young cactus shoots. If you have access to these – or can located canned *nopalitos* – substitute them for the green beans.

INGREDIENTS

4 cups cut green beans

2 tomatoes, peeled, seeded and chopped

½ small onion, minced

2 or 3 drained pickled jalapeño chiles, seeded and sliced into strips

romaine leaves, to serve

crumbled fresh cheese, for the garnish

DRESSING

2 tbsp wine vinegar

1 tbsp freshly chopped cilantro

large pinch dried oregano

3 tbsp olive oil

salt and pepper

Make the dressing. Mix the vinegar, cilantro and dried oregano in a small bowl. Whisk in the olive oil, then add salt and pepper to taste.

Combine the beans, tomatoes, onion, and jalapeños in a bowl. Add the dressing and toss lightly.

Line a salad bowl with the romaine leaves. Spoon the dressed salad into the center and garnish with the crumbled fresh cheese.

COOK'S TIP

Use feta cheese for the garnish, if you like. It isn't remotely authentic, but tastes delicious with the beans and chiles.

POTATOES WITH CHILE, PEANUTS, AND CHEESE

Serves 4

Roast potatoes with a difference: adding onion, garlic, and chiles creates a sensational dish and the roasted peanuts on top are an inspirational extra.

INGREDIENTS

4½ cups finely diced potatoes

1 large onion, sliced

2 garlic cloves, chopped

5 red fresno chiles

4 to 5 tbsp olive oil

salt and pepper

1 cup shelled raw peanuts

shavings of grated Parmesan cheese

Preheat the oven to 400°F. Put the potatoes in a roasting pan and scatter the onion and garlic over.

Make a slit down each chili and scrape out the seeds and membrane. Chop roughly. Sprinkle over the vegetables, drizzle with the oil, then add the seasoning. Turn the vegetables in the oil until evenly coated. Roast in the oven for 50 minutes, turning the vegetables occasionally.

Scatter the peanuts over and continue to roast until cooked and golden. Transfer to a bowl and serve topped with shavings of Parmesan.

BRAISED OKRA WITH CHILES

Serves 4

Braising okra with onion, chiles, bell pepper, and tomatoes really brings out the flavor of this unusual vegetable.

INGREDIENTS

1 lb okra

2 tbsp sunflower oil

1 large onion, thinly sliced

4 green Anaheim chiles, seeded and sliced

1 green bell pepper, seeded and sliced

1½ cups peeled, seeded and chopped tomatoes

salt and pepper

3 tbsp water

plain yogurt, for serving

Trim the okra and prick each pod a few times with a fork.

Heat the oil in a pan and sauté the onion and chiles for 5 minutes, or until softened. Add the green bell pepper and cook for 2 minutes more.

Stir in the chopped tomatoes, the okra and water, with seasoning to taste. Bring to a boil. Reduce the heat, cover the pan and simmer for 8 minutes, or until the okra is tender. Transfer to a bowl and serve immediately topped with spoonfuls of yogurt.

▶ *(Above) Potatoes with Chile, Peanuts, and Cheese (Below) Braised Okra with Chiles*

RED RICE

Serves 4

INGREDIENTS

2 tbsp sunflower oil

I red onion, chopped

2 garlic cloves, chopped

5 red Anaheim chiles, seeded and chopped

6 sun-dried tomatoes, chopped

3½ to 3¾ cups vegetable stock

I cup long-grain rice

I red bell pepper, seeded and chopped

2 tbsp tomato paste

salt and pepper

¾ cup whole kernel corn

freshly chopped cilantro, for the garnish

Preheat the oven to 350°F. Heat the oil in a pan and gently sauté the onion, garlic, chiles, and sun-dried tomatoes for 3 minutes. Add 1¼ cups of the stock and simmer for 10 minutes, or until the tomatoes are soft. Purée in a food processor, then transfer to a flameproof casserole.

Add the rice and red bell pepper. Mix the tomato paste with 2 tbsp of the remaining stock and stir into the tomato mixture. Add 2 more cups of the stock and seasoning to taste.

Bring to a boil on the hob, then cover and place in the oven. Cook for 30 minutes. Add the corn kernels with extra stock if necessary and cook for 10 minutes more, or until the rice is tender. Separate the grains with a fork and serve sprinkled with the cilantro.

GREEN RICE

Serves 4

INGREDIENTS

2 tbsp sunflower oil

I large onion, chopped

2 garlic cloves, chopped

4 green Anaheim chiles, seeded and sliced

I cup long-grain rice

I green bell pepper, seeded and chopped

2½ cups vegetable stock

salt and pepper

¾ cup frozen peas

I tbsp freshly chopped parsley

2 tbsp pumpkin seeds, toasted

Heat the oil in a large, deep skillet and sauté the onion, garlic, and chiles for 3 minutes. Stir in the rice and green bell pepper, and sauté for 3 minutes more.

Pour in the stock and bring to a boil. Reduce the heat and simmer for 15 minutes, or until the rice is almost tender. Add a little more stock if necessary and stir occasionally during cooking.

Stir in the peas and seasoning to taste, and cook for 5 to 7 minutes more, or until the rice and peas are cooked. Adjust the seasoning and serve sprinkled with the parsley and toasted pumpkin seeds.

◀ *Above: Red Rice, Below: Green Rice*

FRAGRANT MUSHROOMS AND PEAS

Serves 4

Mushrooms yield quite a lot of liquid when sautéed. It is important to keep the heat under the pan fairly high so that this is driven off and the mixture is quite dry.

INGREDIENTS

4 to 5 cups button mushrooms

2 tbsp oil

1 small onion, finely sliced

¼ tsp cumin seeds, crushed

¼ tsp mustard seeds

2 tomatoes, chopped

1 fresh green chile, minced

1 cup frozen peas

½ tsp chili powder

¼ tsp turmeric

½ tsp salt

1 small red bell pepper, seeded and chopped

4 fat garlic cloves, minced

2 tbsp freshly chopped cilantro

chopped scallions or chives, for the garnish

Cut the small mushrooms into halves and the larger ones into quarters. Heat the oil in a pan and sauté the onions gently for 5 minutes. Add the cumin and mustard seeds and sauté for 2 to 3 minutes more.

Stir in the tomato and green chile, followed by the mushrooms and peas. Stir-fry them for 2 to 3 minutes over medium heat.

Add the chili powder, turmeric and salt, mixing well. Cook, uncovered for 5 to 7 minutes.

Finally, stir in the bell pepper, garlic and cilantro and cook for 5 minutes more, until the mixture is quite dry. Garnish with the scallions or chives.

EGGPLANT WITH POTATOES AND CHILES

Serves 4 to 6

INGREDIENTS

1 eggplant
2 potatoes
2 tbsp oil
½ onion, sliced
½ tsp cumin seeds
½ tsp roasted coriander seeds
3 to 4 curry leaves (optional)
1 tsp grated fresh gingerroot
4 to 5 garlic cloves, finely chopped
½ tsp chili powder
¼ tsp turmeric
salt to taste
1 tbsp plain yogurt
½ tsp sugar
1 to 2 fresh green chiles, chopped
¾ cup water
1 green bell pepper, seeded and chopped
1 tomato, chopped
1 tbsp lemon juice
2 tbsp freshly chopped cilantro

Cut the eggplant into quarters lengthwise, then, holding the pieces together, cut them across into ½-inch chunks.

Scrub the potatoes thoroughly, but do not peel them. Cut each one into 12 bite-size pieces.

Heat the oil in a heavy saucepan and sauté the onion for about 7 minutes until golden brown. Add the cumin and coriander seeds, with the curry leaves, if using. Fry for 1 to 2 minutes, then add the ginger, half the garlic, the chili powder, turmeric, and salt. Cook this mixture over a high heat for about 2 minutes, adding 2 tbsp of the water if necessary so that the spice paste does not stick to the pan.

Add the eggplant then stir in the yogurt, sugar, and green chiles. Cook for 2 to 3 minutes. Add the remaining water, cover tightly, reduce the heat and simmer for 15 minutes.

Add the potato, bell peppers, and tomato. Replace the lid and simmer for 10 minutes more. Checking the mixture, add a little more water if needed. Lastly, add the remaining garlic, the lemon juice, and the cilantro. Cook for 1 minute more, gently stir to mix thoroughly, then serve.

SAUCES & SALSAS

GREEN CHILI SAUCE

Makes about 2 cups

Ideal to serve with egg dishes, chicken, or as the basis of a stew or casserole.

INGREDIENTS

1 lb fresh green Anaheim chiles

1 large onion, quartered

3 garlic cloves, peeled

2 tbsp corn oil or olive oil

1¼ cups chicken or vegetable stock

1 tsp salt

½ tsp black pepper

2 tbsp freshly chopped cilantro

thinly sliced fresh chile, for the garnish

Preheat the broiler. Place the chiles, onion, and garlic in the broiler pan and drizzle with the oil. Broil for 5 to 8 minutes, or until the chiles have blistered and the skins blackened. Put the chiles into a plastic bag and leave to sweat for about 10 minutes, then rub off the skins.

Put the chiles with all the other ingredients into a food processor, except the cilantro. Process to a chunky purée. Stir in the cilantro and warm through just before serving. Garnish with the sliced chile.

RED CHILI PASTE

Makes about 1½ cups

Use when extra heat is required in order to spice up soups, stews, and casseroles.

INGREDIENTS

4 red habanero chiles, seeded

1 onion, chopped

2 garlic cloves, crushed

2 tsp ground coriander

1 tbsp freshly chopped cilantro

1-inch piece gingerroot, peeled and grated

grated peel and juice of 2 limes

1 tsp salt

½ tsp black pepper

3 tbsp corn oil or olive oil

Rinse the chiles and put them in the top of a steamer over a pan of gently steaming water. Steam for 5 minutes or until soft. Alternatively, cover with hot water and leave for 15 minutes, then drain.

Put all the ingredients into a food processor and blend to a thick paste, adding a little extra oil if necessary. Transfer to a screw-top jar and store in the refrigerator. Use within 1 week.

▶ *(Clockwise from top left): Red Chili Paste, Chili Pepper Relish, Green Chili Sauce, Red Chili Sauce*

RED CHILI SAUCE

Makes about 1½ cups

Both Green and Red Chili Sauce are used as a condiment for fish, meat, and poultry or can be used as a dip.

INGREDIENTS

3 red serrano chiles
1 tbsp corn oil or olive oil
4 ripe tomatoes, peeled, seeded, and chopped
4 shallots, finely chopped
2 garlic cloves, chopped
1 tsp ground cumin
1 tsp ground coriander
⅔ cup vegetable or chicken stock
2 tbsp tomato paste
½ tsp salt
½ tsp black pepper
1 tbsp lime juice
2 tbsp freshly chopped cilantro

Preheat the broiler. Place the chiles in the broiler pan and drizzle with the oil. Broil for 5 minutes, or until blackened and blistered. Put into a plastic bag and leave to sweat for 10 minutes, then rub off the skins and chop the flesh.

Put all the ingredients, except the cilantro, into a food processor and blend to a thick purée. Pour into a skillet and cook over gentle heat, stirring frequently, for 10 minutes.

CHILI AND ANCHOVY SAUCE

Serves 4 to 6

This Thai sauce is not very spicy, but has an interesting combination of flavors.

INGREDIENTS

6 garlic cloves

1 tbsp sliced shallot

1 tsp chopped fresh gingerroot

2 tbsp finely chopped anchovies

1 tbsp lemon juice

1 dried red chile, pounded finely

1 kaffir lime leaf, torn into small pieces

½ lemongrass stalk, outer leaves removed, finely sliced

Dry-fry the garlic, shallot, and ginger in a nonstick skillet for 3 minutes, then chop finely. Pound with the rest of the ingredients using a mortar and pestle on a spice mill.

MEXICAN TOMATO SAUCE

Makes about 6 cups

Use this rich sauce with tortillas, over pasta, with broiled meat or even as a topping for steamed cauliflower.

INGREDIENTS

2 to 3 tbsp olive oil

2 large onions, finely chopped

3 or 4 garlic cloves, chopped

2 to 4 serrano chiles, chopped

24-oz can tomatoes, chopped

6-oz can tomato paste

¾ cup red wine

1 tbsp freshly chopped herbs (parsley, sage, rosemary, thyme, oregano)

salt and pepper

sugar to taste (optional)

2 tbsp freshly chopped cilantro

Heat the oil in a pan. Add the onions and garlic and sauté for 5 to 8 minutes, until they are soft and golden. Add the chiles, tomatoes, tomato paste, wine, herbs and seasoning. Add sugar if the sauce is too sharp; this will depend on the wine and the tomatoes, and may not be necessary. Simmer for 15 to 30 minutes. Stir in the cilantro before serving.

HOT HOT HOT PEPPER SAUCE

Makes about 2 cups

INGREDIENTS

1 cup vinegar

7 tbsp lime or lemon juice

2 onions, minced

6 radishes, finely chopped

2 garlic cloves, minced

2 to 3 tbsp minced fresh hot chile

4 tbsp olive oil

salt and pepper

Mix all the ingredients in a non-reactive bowl and serve. Store any leftover sauce in a tightly sealed glass jar.

SPICY GROUND BEEF SAUCE

Serves 4

Kenyan chiles could be used in this sauce if available, for a milder flavor. Use in tacos, enchiladas or burritos,

INGREDIENTS

1 tbsp corn oil, or olive oil

1 onion, finely chopped

2 garlic cloves, crushed

2 Scotch Bonnet chiles, seeded and chopped

2 celery stalks, trimmed and finely chopped

12 oz ground beef

1 tbsp tomato paste mixed with 2 tbsp water

1½ cups peeled and chopped ripe tomatoes

1 tsp ground coriander

1 tsp ground cumin

2 tbsp cider vinegar

1 tsp honey

2 tbsp freshly chopped oregano

Heat the oil in a skillet and sauté the onion, garlic, chiles, and celery for 5 minutes. Add the beef and cook, stirring frequently, for 5 to 8 minutes, or until browned.

Stir in the tomato paste mixture, with all the remaining ingredients. Bring to a boil, then reduce the heat and simmer for 45 minutes, or until the sauce is thick and flavorsome.

AVOCADO SALSA

Makes about 2 1/2 cups

Avocado salsa is similar to guacamole, but the avocado is cubed rather than mashed, and is mixed with minced chiles. Use it as a dip for chips or a topping for chili. You can mix the other ingredients in advance, but do not dice and add the avocados until just before serving. Remove the seeds and veins from the jalapeño chiles for a milder salsa.

INGREDIENTS

1 medium tomato, diced

1/2 medium red onion, finely chopped

2 fresh jalapeño chiles, minced

3 tbsp lime juice

1 tbsp olive oil

1 tbsp freshly chopped cilantro

salt and pepper

3 avocados diced

Combine the tomato, onion, chiles, lime juice, olive oil and cilantro in a bowl. Season to taste. Cover and set aside for several hours to allow the flavors to blend, if you have time. Cut the avocados in half and remove the peel and seeds. Dice all the flesh and gently stir it into the salsa just before serving.

PINEAPPLE SALSA

Serves 4

INGREDIENTS

3/4 to 1 cup pineapple juice

1 garlic clove, chopped

1 green onion, thinly sliced

1 ripe tomato, finely chopped, or 1/4 cup canned tomato juice or crushed tomatoes

1 tbsp freshly chopped mint

1 tbsp freshly chopped cilantro

hot pepper sauce, to taste

dash each of ground cumin and sugar

juice of 1/2 lime plus a little of the grated peel

salt

Mix all the ingredients in a bowl, cover and let rest for 30 minutes to allow the flavors to develop.

▶ *Avocado Salsa*

PICKLES & CHUTNEYS

GARLIC AND CHILI EXTRACT

A few drops of this extract really perks up soups and stews, but because the flavor is very intense, it should be used with caution. The quantities of garlic and chiles listed are merely a guide and may vary, depending on the size of the bottle selected, and on personal taste.

INGREDIENTS

10 garlic cloves

5 small fresh green chiles

cooking sherry

Peel the garlic cloves and cut them in half. Prick the chiles all over. Mix them together and pack into a clean, dry wine bottle.

Cover with the sherry and fill the bottle, leaving room for the cork. Cork the bottle securely and leave, undisturbed, in a cool, dark place for a couple of weeks.

The sherry can be topped up from time to time.

COOK'S TIP
A bottle of this extract makes a great gift for a keen cook. Use pale sherry for the best effect, and label the bottle with a warning that the contents should be used with care.

INDONESIAN HOT VEGETABLE PICKLE

Serves 4

Peanuts and pineapple are pepped up with chile in this spicy pickle. It is often served with curries, cold meat, or even fish dishes.

INGREDIENTS

4 fresh red Thai chiles

1 large onion, chopped

3 garlic cloves

2 cups fresh roasted peanuts

3 tbsp sunflower oil

3 tbsp sugar

2½ cups white wine vinegar

1½ cups cut green beans

1 cucumber, peeled and diced

2 red bell peppers, seeded and chopped

1½ cups small cauliflower flowerets

1 fresh pineapple, flesh removed from shell, cored and diced

salt and pepper

a few threads of saffron or ½ tsp turmeric

Put the chiles, onion, and garlic into a food processor and process until smooth. Reserve. Grind or process the peanuts until lightly chopped and reserve.

Heat the oil in a large pan and gently cook the chili purée for 4 minutes. Add the sugar and vinegar, bring to a boil, then lower the heat and simmer for 5 minutes.

Add the peanut paste and then the vegetables and pineapple with the seasoning and saffron or turmeric. Simmer for 2 minutes, stirring constantly. If serving hot, heat through gently for 4 to 5 minutes, stirring frequently. If serving cold, heat through for 2 minutes, then place in a serving dish, cover and chill. Stir thoroughly before serving.

If stored in sealed screw-top glass jars, the pickle can be kept in the refrigerator or a cool place for up to 1 month.

▶ *Garlic and Chili Extract*

CORN AND CHILI RELISH

Makes about 4 cups

The corn kernels used to make this light, unthickened relish should either be freshly cut or frozen; canned kernels would not hold their shape. You can either use the relish immediately or you can bottle it for use within two months.

INGREDIENTS

2 fresh green or red chiles

1 green bell pepper

1 cup whole corn kernel

2 tbsp sugar

½ tsp salt

¼ tsp mustard powder

2 cups white wine vinegar

Remove the seeds from the chiles and finely chop them. Core, seed, and finely chop the bell pepper. Put the chiles and bell peppers into a non-reactive saucepan and add the corn.

In a bowl, mix together the sugar, salt, and mustard powder. Gradually stir in the vinegar, then pour the mixture into the pan. Bring to a boil, then lower the heat and simmer for 15 minutes, or until the corn is just tender.

Let the relish cool completely. Serve immediately or store in a covered container in the refrigerator for use within one week. Alternatively, spoon it, while still warm, into warm, sterilized jars and seal immediately. Once opened, use within 1 week.

CARIBBEAN MANGO CHUTNEY

Makes about 5 lb

Very dark in color, this is a rich, hot and fruity chutney that still retains the fresh mango taste. Leave it for two weeks before opening. Once opened, it will keep for up to one month. Unopened, it will keep for up to two years.

INGREDIENTS

6 under-ripe mangoes

1 tbsp salt

2 oz dried tamarind

6 tbsp boiling water

1½ cups raisins, soaked for 12 hours

3 cups malt vinegar

2 oz fresh gingerroot, peeled and grated

2 fresh red or green chiles, seeded and finely chopped

2 garlic cloves, minced

1¾ cups soft dark sugar

Peel and dice the mangoes. Put them into a bowl, stir in the salt, and leave them for 2 hours. Do not drain them. Put the tamarind into a bowl, pour the boiling water over it and leave for 30 minutes. Drain the tamarind, rubbing the pulp through the strainer into a small bowl.

Put the raisins into a preserving pan or non-reactive saucepan. Add the vinegar, mangoes, tamarind pulp, ginger, chiles, garlic, and sugar. Bring to a boil, lower the heat and simmer for about 1 hour, or until the mixture is thick. The mangoes should be tender but still in recognizable pieces.

Spoon the hot chutney into warm, sterilized jars and seal immediately.

PICKLED PEARS WITH CHILES

Makes about 4 lb

Tender, mildly spiced slices of pear in a sharp-sweet pickle are an excellent way to make use of cheap and plentiful fruit in the fall. Keep the pickle for one week before using. Unopened, it will keep for up to six months. Once opened, it must be eaten within one week.

INGREDIENTS

1 cinnamon stick, broken

6 cloves

1-inch piece fresh gingerroot, bruised

2½ cups white wine vinegar

3 cups sugar

6 small pears (about 4 lb)

dried red chiles, one for each jar

Tie the cinnamon, cloves, and gingerroot in a small piece of cheesecloth. Put the spice bag into a non-reactive saucepan with the vinegar and sugar. Set the pan over low heat and stir until the sugar has dissolved. Bring the syrup to a boil and remove the pan from the heat.

Bring a saucepan of water to a boil. Meanwhile, peel and quarter the pears and cut out their cores. Cook the pears in the boiling water for 5 minutes, then drain them.

Bring the syrup to a boil again and add the pears. Reduce the heat down and simmer for about 15 minutes, until they are tender but still firm and they look translucent.

Using a slotted spoon, lift the pears out of the syrup and pack them into warm, sterilized jars. Put one dried chile into each jar.

Lift out the spice bag from the syrup and boil the syrup again for about 5 minutes. Pour the hot syrup over the pears. Seal immediately.

TOMATO AND GREEN PEPPER RELISH

Makes about 2½ lb

Good with burgers, sausages and all barbecue food, this rich tomato relish can be served immediately or it can be kept in a covered container in the refrigerator for up to two weeks.

INGREDIENTS

8 tomatoes

4 tbsp olive oil

1 onion, finely chopped

1 garlic clove, minced

1 green bell pepper, cored, seeded and diced

1 or 2 small fresh green chiles, seeded and diced (optional)

2 tbsp soft dark brown sugar

4 tbsp malt vinegar

Put the tomatoes into a large heatproof bowl. Pour boiling water over them and leave for 1 minute. Drain and skin them.

Heat the oil in a saucepan over low heat. Cook the onion and garlic for 2 minutes, then stir in the bell peppers and chiles and cook for 2 minutes more, stirring occasionally, until they begin to soften.

Increase the heat up to medium and add the tomatoes. Stir until heated through, then stir in the sugar. When it has melted, add the vinegar and bring it to a boil. Remove the pan from the heat and let the relish cool completely.

▶ *Pickled Pears with Chiles*

PICCALILLI

Makes about 6 lb

Almost any combination of crunchy vegetables can be used to make this mustard pickle, but the selection below
works very well. Leave the pickle for one week before using. Unopened, it will keep for up to three months.
Once opened, it should be eaten within two weeks.

INGREDIENTS

1 large cucumber
6 zucchini (about 1 lb)
1 large cauliflower (about 2 lb)
4 onions
2 tbsp salt
3¾ cups vinegar
1 tbsp mustard seeds
1 tsp black peppercorns
4 dried red chiles
⅔ cup soft brown sugar
2 tsp ground ginger
1 tbsp ground turmeric
1 tbsp mustard powder
2 tsp flour

Wipe but do not peel the
cucumber; cut it into ½-inch
dice. Wipe the zucchini and thinly slice
them. Divide the cauliflower into small
flowerets. Chop the onions.

Put all the chopped vegetables into
a large bowl and add the salt. Toss well.
Leave for 12 hours. Drain the
vegetables in a colander, rinse them

through with cold water and drain
them again.

Pour 2½ cups of the vinegar into a
non-reactive saucepan and add the
mustard seeds, peppercorns, and
chiles. Bring to a boil, reduce the heat,
cover and simmer for 10 minutes.
Strain the vinegar and return it to
the saucepan.

Put the ginger, turmeric, mustard
powder, and flour into a small bowl
and gradually mix in the remaining
vinegar. Stir the mixture into the hot
vinegar in the saucepan. Bring the
mixture to a boil and stir in the
vegetables. Reduce the heat and
simmer for 10 minutes, stirring
occasionally.

Let the pickle cool completely then
pack it into cold, sterilized jars. Seal the
jars immediately.

SWEET SPICED ONION SLICES

Makes about 5 lb

Dried chiles and cloves flavor this sweet onion pickle. Small button mushrooms can be pickled in the same way: peel them and salt them whole, then proceed with the recipe as for sliced onions. Leave the pickle for one week before using. Unopened, it will keep for up to four months but once opened, it should be eaten within one week.

INGREDIENTS

12 onions (about 3 lb)

2 tbsp salt

2½ cups white wine vinegar

1 cup sugar

1 tbsp cloves

12 dried red chiles

Slice the onions very thinly into rings. Layer them in a bowl with the salt, cover and leave for 12 hours. Rinse the onions with cold water and drain them well.

Put the vinegar, sugar, cloves, and chiles into a non-reactive saucepan and stir them over a low heat until the sugar has melted. Bring to a boil, reduce the heat and simmer gently for 5 minutes.

Pack the onions into warm, sterilized jars. Pour the hot vinegar over them, ensuring the cloves and chiles are evenly distributed among the jars. Seal immediately.

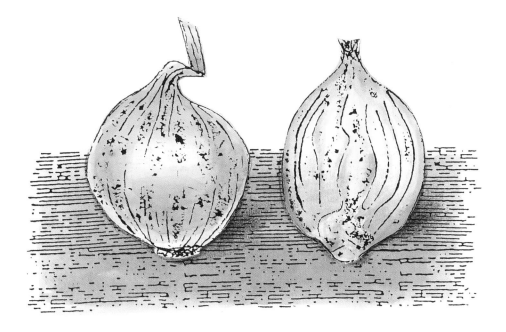

GARLIC AND CHILI JELLY

This is a very good relish with roasts and cold cuts. Its clear color and excellent flavor make it a good candidate for the food stand at a fundraiser.

INGREDIENTS

4 lb sour apples

2 heads garlic (about 25 cloves)

10 small fresh red chiles

5 cups water

sugar (see method)

Cut the apples into 1-inch chunks, but do not peel or core them. Separate and peel the garlic cloves and cut each in half lengthwise. Cut the chiles in half.

Put the apples, garlic, and chiles into a kettle pan with the water and stew for about 1 hour, until the apples are reduced to pulp. Tip into a jelly bag, or thick cloth, and leave to drain overnight. Do not be tempted to speed up the flow of juice by squeezing the bag, as this will only make the juice cloudy.

Measure the juice into a clean pan and add 2 cups sugar for every 2½ cups of liquid. Stir over gentle heat until the sugar has dissolved. Boil rapidly for 10 minutes, until a little of the jelly sets when cooled on a plate, and wrinkles when you push it with your finger.

While the jelly is still hot, pour it into dry, warmed jars, filling them almost to the brim. Cover the surface of the jelly with a disk of wax paper. Put a cellophane or wax paper cover over each jar, secure with thin twine or an elastic band, and store in a dark, cool, dry place.

INDEX

A

Anaheim chiles 9
ancho chiles 9
Anchovies, Crispy 54
Anchovy Sauce, Chile 176
arbol chiles 9
Arroz con Pollo 86
Avocado & Chicken Soup 44
Avocado Salsa 178
Avocado Soup, Cold 39

B

banana chiles 9
Beancurd, Spiced Vegetables with 142
Bean Dip with Chile 20
Bean Salad, with Pickled Jalepeños 165
Beans, Mixed Masala 146
Bean-Sprout Salad 161
Beef, & Salsa Chili, Simple 115
Beef, Quick Cook, with Beancurd
    & Vegetables 111
Beef, Stir-Fried with Garlic & Chiles 109
Beef-Curry, Coconut 108
Beef Hotpot with Chili Marinade 107
Beef Sauce, Spicy Ground 177
bird's-eye chiles 11
Bisteck Ranchero 106
Black-eyed Peas in Ginger Sauce 135
Bredie 119
Brie, Deep-Fried, with Spicy Apricot Salsa
    59
Burgers, Chile Rice 151

C

Callaloo 46
Cauliflower & Tomato Curry 136
cayenne 9
    powder 12
Cellophane Noodles with Vegetables 150
Chalupas 24
Cheese-filled Chiles in Batter Jackets 138
Cheese Turnovers with Green-Tomato
    Sauce 152
Chicken, Jamaican 81
Chicken, Marinated Broiled 94
Chicken, Spatchcocked, with Chili
    Sauce 87
Chicken, Spiced, with Green Peppers 90
Chicken, Stir-fried 82
Chicken, Vietnamese Broiled 93
Chicken, White Chili with 10
Chicken & Avocado Soup 44
Chicken with Chickpeas 91
Chicken & Chile Soup 43
Chicken & Chiles in Sour Cream Sauce 80
Chicken Fried with Cashew Nuts 95
Chicken Kabobs with Chili Sauce 85

Chicken with Pine Nuts, Chile 84
Chicken in Red Chili & Tomato Sauce 92
Chicken Soup, Spicy 45
Chicken Wings, Barbecued 89
Chicken Wings, Chili-Tequila 88
Chile con Queso 20
Chile-Pepper Relish 28
Chili-Rice Burgers 151
Chiles
    drying 14
    as garnish 15
    handling 15
    roasting 14
Chiles, Hot Stuffed 60
chili flakes 12
chili oils 13
chili paste 13
    Red 174
Chili with Peaches & Three Beans 139
chili powders 12
chili sauces 13
    Chili & Anchovy 176
    Green 174
    Red 175
chipotle chiles 9
Chocolate Sauce, Turkey in 102
Coconut-Beef Curry 108
Coconut & Ginger Soup 38
Congo chiles 9
Corn & Chile Relish 184
Corn Salad with Roasted Chiles & Peppers
    162
Cornbread, Skillet, with Bacon & Jalapeños
    33
Crab Cakes, Korean, with Ginger Dipping
    Sauce 51
Crab-Stuffed Tomatoes 56
Cucumber Salad with Chiles 163

D

de agua chiles 9
Duck, Roast, with Chiles 99
Duck Breasts with Pumpkin Seeds 97
Duck in Green Chili Sauce 96
Duck with Two Sauces 98
Dutch chiles 9

E

Eggplant with Potatoes & Chiles 171
Eggplant Purée, Spiced 22
Eggs, Fried, in a Spiced Vegetable Nest 155
Eggs, Ranch Style 157
Empanadas 30
Enchiladas, Vegetarian 28

F

Fajitas, Beef 116

Feijoada 129
Fish, Fried, with Chili Topping 71
Fish, Mixed, Creole Style 76
Fish, Steamed, with Lemon & Chile 70
Fish, Yogurt-Spiced 68
Fish with Black Beans 66
Fish Pâté, Hot & Smoky 23
Fish Soup with Chiles 40
Fish Strips, Fried, with Chile Dipping Sauce
    34
fresno chiles 10

G

Garlic & Chili Extract 182
Garlic & Chili Jelly 190
Green Chili Sauce 174
Guacamole 18
guajillo chile 10

H

habanero chile 10
Ham, Braised, with Chili Sauce
    131
honka (hontaka) chile 10
Hors d'oeuvres, Thai 19
Hot Hot Hot Pepper Sauce 177
Hot Shrimp Soup 40
Hungarian cherry chiles 10
Hungarian sweet chiles 10

I

Indonesian-Hot Vegetable Pickle
    182

J

jalapeño chiles 10
Jamaican Chicken 81
Jamaican hot chiles 10
jerk seasoning 13

K

kalyanpur chiles 10
Kashmir chiles 10
Kashmiri Lamb 121
Kenyan chiles 10
kesanakurru chiles 10
Kitchen-Sink Chili 117
Korean chiles 11
    powder 12
Korean Crab Cakes with Ginger Dipping
    Sauce 51
kovilpatt chiles 10

L

Lamb, in Spicy Yogurt Sauce 120
Lamb, Ground with Cauliflower 112
Lamb, New Mexico Chili with 122

Lamb, Stewed, with Habaneros 123
Lentil & Vegetable Chili 141
Lettuce Packages, Thai 58

M
Mango Chutney, Caribbean 185
Mango Salad, Green 160
Marinated Broiled Chicken 94
Meatloaf, Spicy 113
Mexican Mini-Meatballs 55
Mexican Tomato Sauce 176
Mixed Leaves with Chipotle Chile Dressing 164
mulato chiles 11
Mushroom Masala Omelet 154
Mushrooms & Peas, Fragrant 170
Mushrooms, Sautéed, with Chili Salsa 56

N
New Mexico chiles 11

O
Okra & Bean Curry 140
Okra, Braised, with Chiles 166
Okra, Shrimp with 72
Omelet, Mushroom Masala 154
Onion Slices, Sweet-Spiced 189

P
Pancakes, Zucchini & Chile 156
paprika 12
pasilla chiles 11
Pasta with Spicy Tomato Sauce 147
Pepper Pizza, Spicy 27
Picadillo 110
Piccalilli 188
Pickle, Indonesian Hot Vegetable 182
Pickled Pears with Chiles 186

Pineapple Salsa 178
poblano chiles 11
Pork & Chili Balls 130
Pork Chili with Smoked Paprika 125
Potato Curry 145
Potato Patties, Spicy 31
Potatoes with Peanuts & Cheese 166
prik chee fa chiles 11

Q
Quesadillas with Refried Beans 26
Quick-Jerk Pork Chops 126

R
Red-Chili Paste 174
Red-Chili Sauce 175
red-pepper (powder) 12
Red Pepper & Chile Soup 47
Refried Beans, Quesadillas with 26

S
Salmon Steaks with Thai-Style Sauce 69
Salsas
    Apricot 59
    Avocado 178
    Pineapple 178
    Tomato 35
Samosas, Spinach & Potato 140
Samosas, Vegetable 32
santaka chiles 11
Scallops with Habanero & Mango Slices 52
Scorcher Chili 114
Scotch Bonnet chiles 11
Seafood Gumbo 77
serrano chiles 11
Shrimp, Deep-Fried, with Spicy Tomato Salsa 35
Shrimp Curry, Goan 74
Shrimp with Okra 72
Shrimp Rellenos 52

Shrimp Soup, Hot & Sour 40
Spicy Brown Rice 148
Spicy Liver Salad 118
Spinach & Potato Samosas 140
Squid, Stir-Fried, with Chiles & Vegetables 75
Squid with Hot-Pepper Sauce 67
Szechuan Noodles with Pork and Chiles 127
Szechuan Hot-Chili Pork 125

T
tabasco 11
    sauce 13
Thai chiles 11
Thai Lettuce Packages 58
Thai Noodles, Fried, with Chiles 148
Tomato & Green-Pepper Relish 186
Tomato Sauce, Mexican 176
Tomato Sauce, Spicy, Pasta with 147
Tomatoes, Crab-Stuffed 56
Tortilla Soup 42
Turkey Chili, Ground, with Black Beans 101
Turkey in Chocolate Sauce 102

V
Vegetable Crunch, Spicy 134
Vegetable Samosas 32
Vegetables in Green Masala, Seasonal 145
Vegetables, Spiced, with Bean Curd 142
Vietnamese Broiled Chicken 93

W
White Chili with Chicken 100

Y
Yogurt-Spiced Fish 68

Z
Zucchini & Chili Pancakes 156

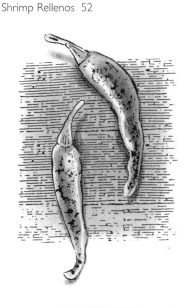